The New World Order Is The Old World Order

By

George Radanovich

Copyright © 2011 by George Radanovich

The New World Order is the Old World Order
by George Radanovich

Printed in the United States of America

ISBN 9781613792636

All rights reserved solely by the author. The author guarantees all contents are original and do not infringe upon the legal rights of any other person or work. No part of this book may be reproduced in any form without the permission of the author. The views expressed in this book are not necessarily those of the publisher.

Unless otherwise indicated, Bible quotations are taken from the King James version.

www.xulonpress.com

Dedicated to the memory of the love of my life

Ethie Weaver Radanovich

and

to our beloved son

King

Table of Contents

Acknowledgements ix

Introduction xi

1. The Four Separations 15

2. The Institutions 32
   The Great Seal 32
   The Design of the Seal 34
   Discovering the Four Institutions 37
   The Four Institutions Were Designed
      to Work Together 41
   Why We Need the Institutions Now
      More Than Ever 45
   Restoring the Four Institutions 47

3. The Institution Of Faith 51
   The Free Exercise of Religion 56
   Follow the Charity Money 61
   The Ass-Backward Faith Based Initiative 62
   Not Off the Hook 65

4. The Institution Of Family 69
   How the Family Prepares Kids 72
   Family and the Individual 77
   Family and Society 83

5. The Institution Of Work 89
   Business and the Individual 94
   Business and Society 100

6. The Institution Of Government 106
   Government and Society 111
   Government and the Individual 119

7. A New Social Contract 126
   The Pursuit of Happiness
     and the Four Institutions 126
   New Contract 136

8. Implementing The Contract 138
   Outclass Government 139
   Rekindle the Independence Machine 142
   Rebuild the Family 149
   Obtain Standing in the Courts 154

Conclusion 159

Acknowledgements

I first want to acknowledge and thank Fred Bigler for teaching me the four institutions. That began a thirty year journey to learn more about the Cultural Mandate and what great relevance it has for our country today. His life is an inspiration.

I also want to thank John McCamman, my former Chief of Staff in Congress. John is an anarchist and doesn't believe any of this, but it didn't keep him from pushing this agenda many years ago in Congress. Throughout our time in Mariposa County government and in the United States Congress, he's been a great mentor, advisor and friend.

For editing assistance and advice on how to move this concept forward I wish to acknowledge and thank John Gizzi and Carlos Rodriguez.

I also want to thank Kasey Pipes, who helped me get thoughts and ideas into coherent sentences and stories. And to Skip Strathearn, who helped with the finishing touches.

Lastly, to George and Joan Radanovich, my parents, for giving me a strong foundation in life.

Introduction

In his book, *Reflections for Ragamuffins*, Brennan Manning says that life is "the parable of the Father unraveling the riddle of existence." Our founding fathers benefited from centuries of political and philosophical discourse that slowly unraveled, revealing tenets that formed the moral foundation of our independence: natural law, the social contract, self-rule and representative government. But revelation didn't stop there. In the 19th century, amidst the clang and clatter of rising humanism and social engineering in many forms, new ideas unraveled that could have guided the world's leading nation of freedom, and the entire West, into a less violent 20th and 21st centuries.

But we missed it.

The New World Order is the Old World Order

Within the last century, the failed world views of communism, fascism, socialism and their American cousin, liberal progressivism, have left in their wake, massive public debt and crumbled institutions.

We are in decline.

This world view bred into all of us, Republican and Democrat, the notion that government alone can now solve all of our problems. The promises of social engineering have left us believing that real change occurs with just a mark on the ballot for the right political candidate. It's all just a matter of giving the power to the right person or the right party. The failure of this world view should be evident to everyone.

The secular humanism spawned by the influence of Karl Marx and Charles Darwin is coming to an end as a legitimate governing force in the Western world. But this demise is creating a vacuum. Which world view will replace it? This is the unspoken anxiety Americans have about our future. Without a new world view to redirect us, America will continue to decline and the only difference between the governance of Democrats and Republicans will be how rapidly the decline occurs.

The New World Order is the Old World Order

Perhaps the answer is not found in some new philosophy, but by looking back. The voice of the 19th Century's more relevant contributor to political thought and natural law was drowned out by his contemporaries. His name was Abraham Kuyper and his old theory of the Cultural Mandate is the "new" world view. His ideas are as relevant and important to today as natural law, the social contract and self-rule was to the founding fathers.

The Cultural Mandate is described in many different ways. Political talk shows talk about the rise from tyranny to freedom. In the world of faith, it is called the restoration of the relationship between mankind and God. It builds slowly over time and the United States of America has a significant role. But in order to keep our role, we must rebuild the institutions that have been decimated by secular humanism and the other destructive isms.

As we learn more about the Cultural Mandate, the way to redeem and restore our country becomes evident. We must replace the old world view of socialism by rebuilding the four institutions established and gifted to us long ago. It begins with our culture, not with politicians in Washington.

My 16 years as a Representative in Congress has shown me that America needs a new world view. These pages further unravel and reveal that new world view. It then presents to the American people a new political spectrum and a new social contract to save our nation.

Chapter One

The Four Separations

In the beginning, God created man in His own image. From the start of mankind, men and women were equipped with the tools needed to live a full life in fellowship with God every day.

God made us on purpose and He made us for a purpose. Have you ever sat in a baseball stadium filled with tens of thousands of people and wondered how God could have an intimate relationship with each and everyone in the ballpark, in the country and even in the world? It is unfathomable but true. No one is too small for God. He knows every person in the world, every hair on their head and He has a distinct purpose and plan for each and every one of them.

Yet the fall of man distorted our relationship to God and our relationship to others. Abusing power and authority

The New World Order is the Old World Order

for thousands of years, people have pursued their own dreams, desires and demands. In short, we've boldly gone after what we wanted and blindly ignored what we needed. The result is not only a broken people, but a broken nation and a broken world.

We have lost our way. But we can find it again.

The story is told of the little boy who kept interrupting his busy father. Exasperated, the father took a nearby newspaper, cut out a map of the world and then ripped it into many pieces. "Here," he said to his son, "go put this map back together."

Within a few minutes, the boy returned, smiling proudly. "I did it", he said as held up the map he had taped back together.

Stunned, the father asked, "How did you do that so fast?"

"It was simple," his son answered. "On the other side of the map there was a photo of a person. I just put the person back together and then the whole world came together."

Yes, we too can put the pieces of our lives back together. And when we do, our nation and our world will make more sense.

We have lost our way. But we can find it again.

The New World Order is the Old World Order

How can we save our country? How can we find our way again? We can create a better future for ourselves, but the path to a bright future requires a serious look back. We can discover where we are going, and how to get there, by looking to our past—not just to the founding of our country, but all the way back to the foundation of the world.

There in the Beginning was a Cultural Mandate. There in the original design of the world, God established the institutions we need to flourish as individuals, not just in our houses of worship, but in our communities and society. The most important institutions were there in the Garden and were reinstated after the Fall. Human history is the story of redemption and these institutions play a key role. By honoring and implementing these institutions we can live our lives in freedom and in a way that redeems our crumbling culture.

We have lost our way. But we can find it again.

In the beginning, God established four institutions so that we could thrive and grow and succeed and we must reacquaint ourselves with them.

The first was faith. We were made a spiritual being. A complete life can only be lived by pursuing a spiritual existence. Our souls long for something more; something better. We need a relationship with a higher power. Faith provides us hope that tomorrow will be better than today. Faith persuades us to do the right thing. Faith opens the door to virtue, independence and charity; critical characteristics for a free society. Faith lights the dark corners of our lives and gives meaning to who we are and what we do. It reminds us that life is not about what we get for ourselves, but about what we give to others.

To live a full life, we must be anchored in faith. Our soul demands it.

Second, God established the family. A complete life is lived within the confines of a family. No man is an island. Everyone needs someone; everyone needs a family. A family provides crucial support at the beginning of life. A family provides the love that sets a strong foundation in life. A family gives help and hope to children and raises future generations. Deep within the soul of every one of us is the need for others. Family meets that need.

To live a full life, we must be anchored in family.

The third institution God established was work. Living a complete life demands that we engage in meaningful work– a vocation. Whether on the top floor or the shop floor, whether on Wall Street or Main Street, the work that we do should be a labor of love. Work should be an outlet for our

God-given talents. Through meaningful work we can create a better world. Work allows us to earn a living, provide for our families and contribute to our country.

To live a full life, we must be anchored in work.

Finally, in acknowledgement of the imperfect world humans have wrought, God established government. Government protects us from enemies abroad. Government enforces law and order at home. The U.S. Constitution said it best, namely that the aim of the newborn government was "to provide for the common defense, promote the general welfare, and secure the blessings of liberty for ourselves and our posterity." For everyone to live a complete life, a proper balance must be struck between our wants and needs and those of others. From the Jewish law found in the Torah all the way up to that of today, governments have sought that balance. And government gives us the security and the protection to live our lives freely and to raise our families.

To live a full life, good government must be instituted.

Faith...family...work...government. Too often, we are oblivious to the Cultural Mandate that can only be implemented by these four institutions. But they were established long ago to provide a firm foundation for living a full and complete life; to protect us, to provide for us and to allow us to flourish.

In public policy, so few of us appreciate the dynamics of these institutions and even fewer actively engage them in the national debate. If God so values these institutions as a means of provision, protection and success in life, should we not know more about how they work? What is their purpose in society? What were they intended to do? What are they intended to provide the individual? Are they in balance? Can we get by without them? What happens to the other institutions when one fails? Can one institution successfully assume the purpose of another?

To reacquaint ourselves with these institutions, let's fast forward from the Garden to the founding of our country, the United States of America.

The famous Revolutionary War era author, Thomas Paine, helped spark the American Revolution when he wrote the pamphlet *Common Sense*. His opening words were, "Writers have so confounded society with government, as to leave little or no distinction between the two; whereas they are not only different, but have different origins." At that time, civilization was emerging from centuries of secular and ecclesiastic tyranny.

Armed with a political philosophy of natural law and self-determination developed over centuries, our founding fathers established a new democracy in America. They took great pains to make sure that government was limited to the protection of life, liberty, and property. That was it. By reigning in government and insuring religious freedom, they created a limited government for limited purposes.

This left the rest of civil society- business, family, and religion— to develop naturally, in accordance with the established mores of America's Judeo-Christian tradition. Without the interference of an overbearing government, the institutions of faith, work and family allowed America to flourish, and the focus on individual freedom led to unprecedented independence in the Western world.

This new liberal democracy was the first opportunity for men and women to live, as Dutch statesman and scholar Abraham Kuyper later said in 1898, "Coram Deo", meaning, before the face of God. He said, "Wherever man may stand, whatever he may do, to whatever he may apply his hand, in agriculture, in commerce, and in industry, constantly standing before the face of his God, he is employed in the service of his God, he has strictly to obey his God, and above all else, he has to aim at the glory of his God."

This was the genius of American freedom—though not perfect, it allowed most Americans to experience His perfect will for their lives, to benefit through the four institutions He provided from the beginning.

In the young America of the late 1700's, the state was reigned in and, with religious freedoms, the remaining institutions of civil society were sound. Some historians speculate that many of the founding fathers thought that once the American government was crafted, the rest of the society "would take care of itself." And it did, for a time. But as the 20th century began, the American culture started to change. Certain institutions thought unchangeable, began to show signs of wear and tear.

The anchor of work began to fail as the Great Depression hit America. At the height of the downturn in the 1930s, the unemployment rate reached 25%. In response, the government stepped in. Much of what Franklin Roosevelt did to save the free enterprise system was intended to be temporary until the markets were restored. Federal Deposit Insurance, for example, merely insured the money people put into banks. Indeed, FDR's policies were under constant attack from the left. Sen. Huey Long (D.-LA) favored a "Share the Wealth" plan that would have re-distributed wealth and ended the free market economy as we had known it. Dr. Francis Townsend, a California physician, devised a concept whereby the federal government would provide every citizen with a monthly pension of $200 per month and that this would be financed by a federal tax on all wholesale and retail sales. The Old Age Revolving Pension Plan, commonly known as the "Townsend Plan," attracted more than 5 million Americans nationwide into Townsend Clubs. Roosevelt's signing of Social Security into law was in part a means of short-circuiting this movement.

Eventually, the economy recovered and with it, the free enterprise system. Though FDR's programs were mild in contrast to those of Long and Townsend, they were made permanent and changed an historic relationship between government and the three other institutions.

FDR and his "New Deal" also orchestrated a dramatic sea change in the role of charity in American society. Up until the Depression, charity in the United States was almost exclusively funded by private sources and, more often than not, run under the aegis of churches. Scottish theologian Thomas Chalmers was an outspoken critic of the relief programs orchestrated in England. From 1819 to 1823, Chalmers oversaw a plan for relief for the poor with the parish of St.

John in Glasgow. All government-funded aid was barred and relief would be met exclusively by contributions of parishioners. As philosopher and social thinker Marvin Olasky noted, "The effects reportedly were remarkable: Church charitable giving increased (donors were confident of the wise use of their money); the better-off induced the poor through habits of industry and thrift to improve their lot; and the number of poor in the parish as a consequence shrank."

By around the middle of the century, charitable societies in every major American city were being established mainly along Chalmers' lines. Workers in these organizations shared a view that the underlying causes and long-term needs of the poor were religious. Only when the poor learned to address these needs would they lift themselves (through God's help) out of poverty.

This changed with the advent of the New Deal and the injection of the federal government into the business of charity and relief. Much of the New Deal programs were struck down by the Supreme Court in the 1930's or completely penciled out of the budget during World War II.

But a seed had clearly been planted and, as Olasky pointed out, "a subtle change in public attitudes toward personal responsibility and rugged individualism was taking place."

In the 1960's, the institutions of family and faith began to change in ways the founding fathers could never have imagined.

The biggest problem was not so much President Lyndon Johnson's prescription for poverty, but his diagnosis. It was wrong. Not long before the "Great Society" and the "War on Poverty," an obscure but brilliant academic had argued that families don't fall apart because they are poor; they are poor because they fall apart. The academic's name was Daniel Patrick Moynihan. But it was 1965 and Moynihan's words stood in conflict with the zeitgeist of the era. No one in Washington seemed to be listening to him. Johnson and too many others thought money was the issue. And so the president spent more and more money on more and more government programs. FDR's Social Security system became a slush fund for the Great Society. It didn't work. "We declared war on poverty and poverty won," joked the Governor of California, Ronald Reagan.

Although he was then a Democrat and one who believed in government intervention to help the helpless, social scientist Irving Kristol voiced doubts about the Great Society; it's massive new programs and its governing philosophy of throwing money at every problem in society. "Unintended consequences" of what he considered the good intentions of Johnson and other Democrats were what concerned Kristol. He believed that the heavy-handedness of the Great Society would breed a culture of dependency, leading to social divisions that would damage the very beneficiaries it was intent on helping. As Kristol wrote as the Great Society was being enacted by Congress, "The legitimate question to ask about any program is 'Will it work?'" He did not believe that the Great Society would work.

Even before his death at age 89, Kristol had been proven a prophet. The Great Society weakened the institution of faith. God was declared dead and a new social contract emerged. In this brave new era of social experimentation, government social programs would replace private charity. Faith was diminished and along with it the virtue, freedom, independence and charity it produces. Charity was gradually transferred to government and became a cold, tax-funded social program producing and expanding a culture of dependence. The long march toward the welfare state began in these years. People started to lean more on the government and less on others. People began to see the government as a first resource and not a last resort. A safety net was built that would eventually trap millions of Americans in a snare and rob them of their best.

Economist Thomas Sowell, himself an African-American, made this case most directly and bluntly, arguing that the Great Society was a major factor in the breakdown of African-American families. "The black family" wrote Sowell, "which had survived centuries of slavery and discrimination, began rapidly deteriorating in the liberal welfare state that subsidized unwed pregnancy and changed welfare from an emergency rescue to a way of life." (Sowell, War on Poverty Revisited, *Capitalism Magazine*, August 17, 2004)

Also, unrest and unease gripped the country in the 1960s. Many young men resisted being drafted to fight in a controversial war in Southeast Asia. Many African-Americans, whose frustrations had been building for years, were enraged when segregation was at least officially banned, but racism and poverty remained. Riots became a common occurrence. Protests against just about everything seemed to be everywhere.

Now celebrating its 50th anniversary, the advent of the birth control pill ushered in the sexual revolution. The results of the counter culture were increasing rates of divorce and abortions. Out of wedlock births, single parenthood and drug use increased.

The New World Order is the Old World Order

The 1960's and the 1970's significantly crippled the institutions of family and faith. They have yet to recover.

Today, as America experiences the early years of a new century, we are living in a very different country than the one given to us by our Founding Fathers. Changes in institutions the Founding Fathers thought unchangeable have radically altered the intended role of government. Today, government is anything but limited and the rest of society isn't the better for it. Today, there is great confusion about the institutions and the roles they are supposed to play. In order to realize the change we are looking for, we need to look at government's role in society and what is expected from family, faith and work to make government perform the way we want it to and the way it should.

We have lost our way. But we can find it again.

We can find it again by re-examining the purposes of these institutions and, redefining the individual's relationship to them. If Thomas Paine were to write *Common Sense* in light of the Cultural Mandate, his opening might well have read; "We have so confounded the institutions of faith, family, government and work as to leave no distinction between the four, yet they are not only different, but have different origins and purposes." For every person to live the American Dream, we must build a wall of separation between church, state, family and business. Their functions must be redefined and reinstituted.

We need to reacquaint ourselves with faith. Faith begins with believing and ends with giving. Faith leads to virtue, which leads to independence and freedom. People who are free and independent give willingly, and this charity changes lives. Individual charity is the rising tide that lifts all boats. A system of charity that taxes to fund government largesse is not charity at all. Only faith that moves the human heart can offer real change. We need to redirect charity. This book will show how.

We need to reinstitute the family. We can't just talk about family values…we have to rebuild the family. This book will show how.

We need to anchor ourselves in work. Business leaders need to do more than make a profit…they need to make a difference. And executives should not only do things right, but do the right thing. The image of duplicity and downright villainy conveyed by Goldman Sachs executives put a human face on business executives who are not doing the right thing for their shareholders. Instead they do in their shareholders. Clearly, this has to change or the alternative will be a greater government hand in the free market system. This book will show how it has to change.

And we need to reduce the role of government. This institution over-taxes, and is over-sized, over-stretched and over-extended.

The government we have today spends too much, taxes too much and is too ineffective. The Federal government is hemorrhaging money. The best, first step to take in fixing a hemorrhage is to apply a tourniquet. This book will show how.

We need to separate the institutions. Confusion about the roles of these institutions continues today even more than at the time of our founding and Americans are suffering because of it. They were established for different purposes, to provide different needs. They must be separate and have limited interaction. There are rules that govern these institutions and this book will explain them.

The Founding Fathers fought the battle against tyranny and won for us democracy. But the struggle to create a more perfect union must continue until every American has the freedom to live life as intended — under the all-seeing eye of a loving God, enjoying life, liberty and happiness through four strong institutions functioning according to their purpose.

The four institutions impact all of our lives all of the time and they are intertwined. We can't address just one. We must address them all. Trying to fix our government without addressing our culture would be like the mechanic who installs new brakes but doesn't fix the transmission. The car can stop, but it won't be able to move. A vehicle and our country need an integrated approach to repairing broken systems.

And so do we. Let's reclaim our country. Let's build the future.

This book looks at the four institutions established at the foundation of time and separating them by purpose will provide the framework for real change in America. This is my theory of institutions and their purpose. And I believe the proper application of it will provide the change we Americans are looking for.

We have lost our way. But we can find it again.

It's not too late. But we need to start now.

Chapter Two

The Institutions

The Great Seal

In 1934, Secretary of Agriculture Henry A. Wallace entered the old State, War and Navy Department Building, next door to the West Wing of the White House. He was there to meet with Cordell Hull, Secretary of State. While in the waiting room, he picked up a book published by the State Department called, *The History of the Seal of the United States*. It was an eye-opening experience. He later wrote:

> Turning to page 53, I noted the colored reproduction of the reverse side of the Seal. The Latin phrase *Novus Ordo Seclorum* impressed me as meaning the New Order of the Ages. I was struck by the fact that

the reverse side of the Great Seal had never been used. Therefore I took the publication to President Roosevelt and suggested a coin be put out with the obverse and reverse sides of the Seal.

Franklin Roosevelt had a lot on his mind in 1934, not the least was the Great Depression, which showed no signs of letting up. Since much of the country still worked in agriculture, FDR always made time for his Agriculture Secretary. But he was perhaps surprised on this day when Henry Wallace spoke not of crops, but of coins. He showed the president the book on the history of the seal. Roosevelt looked it over. He liked the idea of using the reverse side of the Great Seal. But instead of a coin, he recommended printing it on the dollar bill. He soon raised the issue with both his Treasury Secretary and the cabinet. They all agreed. And soon the dollar bill as we now know it—with both sides of the Great Seal of the United States prominently featured on the back—was being produced.

What was it about the seal that so impressed Wallace and Roosevelt? Why did they think it was an important enough issue to take on in the midst of the Great Depression? More importantly, is there anything about the Great Seal that has relevance to us today?

The Design of the Seal

On July 4, 1776, America declared its independence. But it did more than that. Often overlooked in history books is the fact that on the very same day the Continental Congress commissioned the creation of a seal for the new country. Not more than a few hours after approving the Declaration of Independence, the Continental Congress established a committee to get to work designing a seal worthy of the new country. And to demonstrate how important the task was, the Congress appointed some of its very best to serve on the committee—John Adams, Benjamin Franklin and Thomas Jefferson. This *Who's Who* of the Founding Fathers set about to create a new seal to symbolize the new nation.

Ironically, Adams, Franklin and Jefferson came up with a design that none of their fellow Founding Fathers liked. But it did include a motto that would re-emerge later: "E Pluribus Unum, Out of Many, One." With the matter of fighting and winning the revolution taking precedence, the Continental Congress soon set aside discussion of a seal.

But in 1780, the seal returned to the agenda. A new committee was selected. This one consisted of three men, all obscure today, but each nonetheless remarkable: William

Churchill Houston of South Carolina, a professor of mathematics and natural science; James Lovell of Massachusetts, a teacher at the Harvard Latin School whose support of the American Revolution caused his estrangement from his pro-British father; and John Morin Scott of New York, a fiery advocate of independence who co-founded the militant Sons of Liberty to pursue the goal of a free nation by any means possible. Again, the result of their efforts did not impress the Continental Congress. This design was soon tabled.

But the work of these three men—Houston and Lovell the scholars and Scott the militant—would not die. Some features of the second seal would reemerge in the later design: the olive branch, the 13 stars and the shield with red and white stripes.

Then, in 1782, another committee tried and failed to create a seal that Congress could agree upon. Again, some of the work would survive from this draft, including the eagle used in the crest (even though no less a Founding Father than Benjamin Franklin himself wanted a turkey!). Finally, later that same year, the Continental Congress turned to Charles Thomson, the Secretary of the Continental Congress. He was a respected and talented man. With the help of William

The New World Order is the Old World Order

Barton, he created a fourth design that was voted on and approved by Congress on June 20, 1782.

In Thomson's design, the seal consisted of an eagle clutching both arrows and an olive branch with a constellation of 13 stars above. But on the reverse side, Thomson offered an entirely different symbol. And it was this symbol that would one day catch the eye of Henry Wallace and Franklin Roosevelt.

The reverse side showed an eye and a pyramid. As Thomson explained, "The pyramid signifies strength and duration." The date 1776 in Roman numerals was found at the base of the pyramid. Rising from the base were thirteen rows of bricks, one for each of the 13 states. Yet the pyramid appeared unfinished, rising toward Heaven, an earthly work in progress. What began in 1776 would continue until the end of this Age.

On top of the pyramid was "an eye in a triangle, surrounded with a glory." Thus, the Founding Fathers imagined their new nation as one that would look up to God while the eye of God looked down on the new nation. And in case anyone missed their point, the Founders added two inscriptions in Latin, one for the eye and one for the pyramid. Novus Ordo Seclorum (which means "a new order of the ages") read the inscription below the pyramid. This probably came from the poet Virgil, who wrote that "a great order of the ages is born anew." Thomson's report explains, "The words under it signify the beginning of the New American Era, which commences from that date [1776]." This translates to "he had nodded in assent to the things that have been started." The eye would bless the building of the pyramid. Or, as Thomson put it, "The eye over it and the motto allude to the many signal interventions of providence in favor of the American cause."

For all the controversy that would later be engendered by the term "new world order," the truth was that this "new world order" was a description of the oldest world order of all—that chronicled in the Garden of Eden.

Discovering the Four Institutions

"The architects of These States laid their foundations, and passed to further spheres," wrote Walt Whitman a century after America was founded. "What they laid is a work done; as much more remains. Now are needed other architects, whose duty is not less difficult, but perhaps more difficult.

Each age forever needs architects. America is not finished, perhaps never will be; now America is a divine true sketch."

The Founding Fathers, Whitman, Roosevelt and many others have understood importance of design in American society. The Seal is the symbol of a well-constructed ascent from tyranny, not just for America, but of civilization over time. We rise from tyranny and chaos to freedom and self-government. The Great Seal represents a stability and symmetry of design that America has come to miss over the years. For this reason, it is important to take a further look at this symbol and learn more about self-government, freedom, independence, and our American purpose.

The Masonic symbols associated with the Seal, such as bricks, the compass, the square and the trowel, speak of the building of a society, and the structure itself speaks of stability and symmetry. The Founding Fathers were architects, not of a new government, but of a new society, a new order, based on freedom and self-government. In this new order, people would have victory over tyranny and live in freedom. It meant the beginning of an age of life lived below the face of a providential God. Is it any wonder that the Founding Fathers approved this design? It fit perfectly with the message of the Declaration of Independence and the vision of the new nation. And is it any wonder that decades later, in the midst of another national crisis, President Roosevelt invoked the symbol as a means of reminding Americans that Providence was in favor of the American cause?

To develop a design of stability and symmetry, you must approach the project from all four sides. Just as the Great Seal shows four distinct walls working together as one, so our country needs all four of its institutions to provide balance and purpose. The symmetry of the four sided pyramid reflects the contributions of institutions in this ascent, this building process toward freedom and self-government under the all-seeing Eye. The symmetry also shows that all institutions must be equally strong in their purpose not only to provide strength to society but to provide freedom and security for as many citizens possible.

As with any architecture, the blueprint includes guidelines for the construction and maintenance of these institutions. They are:

1. Life, Liberty and the Pursuit of Happiness are attainable for more Americans when the institutions are strong.

2. Americans are best served when each of the institutions operates within its purpose.
3. An institution can temporarily assume the responsibilities of another that is weakened or underperforming.
4. An institution performing the responsibilities of another is always a poor substitute, and individual freedom suffers as a consequence.

Today, we know that Jefferson's description of the inalienable rights to life, liberty and the pursuit of happiness in the Declaration of Independence, and Kuyper's vision of living life "Corem Deo", in the face of God, are milestones in civilization's progress within the Cultural Mandate. Our Founding Fathers' passion for freedom helped put us front and center before the four institutions. Mankind, in a natural state, is free to enjoy a relationship with a Higher Power, and God, as a protector and provider, is able to protect and provide through the four institutions of Faith, Family, Work and Government.

The Great Seal is the symbol of two things, a stable and productive individual life, and four strong institutions functioning according to their purposes, affording access to the American dream for all.

The Four Institutions Were Designed to Work Together

Although we've never considered the Great Seal as such and have never referred to it when building our future, the Founding Fathers actually gave us a blueprint, or a symbol of what a free society looks like. The blueprint calls for four equal walls in the building of the pyramid. These four walls give balance, strength and purpose to the design.

Faith...Family...Work...Government. The four institutions contribute equally to the individual life. A person living in a society where all four institutions are healthy and strong has the greatest opportunity for success in life.

Consider the child's relationship to these four institutions: When family institutions are healthy, a child is more likely to learn respect for his or her parents. When government institutions are healthy, a child is more likely to obey the law. In healthy businesses, a child is more likely to learn the work ethic. In healthy religious institutions, a child is more likely to maintain a clear conscience before his or her God. These make up the foundation of a life well lived.

With a focus on four healthy and equal institutions functioning according to their purpose, we, as a society, can provide to every individual the freedom and security to pursue the promised opportunity for life, liberty, and happiness.

With all four walls, or institutions, the pyramid starts from a firm foundation and rises symmetrically. Weaken just one of the walls and the design of the pyramid is compromised and the structure, society, is weakened. Yet that is exactly what has occurred in this country for the past century—a weakening of our institutions, and thereby a weakening of our country.

During the last 100 years, America's government has become disproportionately large to offset weaknesses in the country's other institutions. The result has been a burdensome governmental structure involved in virtually every aspect of the lives of every American. The New Deal was offered in response to a collapsed financial institution. The fundamental principles of the New Deal, and the Great Society programs thirty years later — the solving of social ills with governmental programs — have resulted in the problems we see all around us today. Of all the money spent by government, 70 percent is controlled at the federal level, while the rest is controlled at the state and local levels. The 537 elected officials in Washington— the President, Vice President, 100 US Senators and 435 US Representatives—have substituted their "wisdom" for the wisdom of the thousands of local elected officials in our communities. As government has grown, influence of the other core institutions has diminished. Their effectiveness has been reduced, creating instability in America. The Era of Big Government will soon be over by collapsing under the heavy weight of debt. The question is, will the three other institutions have the strength to fill the vacuum?

More often than not, a state with its hand in everything—stifling the free market and limiting entrepreneurship as well as basic liberty—collapses under its own weight. Much of the old Communist empire, from the old Soviet Union to its satellite states in Eastern Europe, basically rotted from within. With a shove, the Ba'athist regime of Saddam Hussein in Iraq fell. To be sure, a Communist dictatorship is still in charge in the People's Republic of China and in the "hermit kingdom" of North Korea. But these are the exceptions to the rule. China permits some entrepreneurship, while relentlessly limiting any progress in democratically-chosen government or civil liberties. The winds of change could well blow into China as well as into North Korea, whose despotic rulers have held power in large part by controlling the flow of information into their country.

While the people of the United States have not suffered under abject despotism through the institution of government, the three other institutions have come under heavy assault. Our families have been decimated over the last 30 years by divorce, teen pregnancy, drug abuse, juvenile crime, and failing educational institutions. While freedom to worship is a right enjoyed by all Americans, religious institutions have abdicated their role as the provider of charity, to government, thus creating a society dependent on government largesse. In his book "Bowling Alone," Harvard professor Robert Putnam documented the significant decline in "social capital" and in participation in the civic associations of "civil society." In the political arena, declining voter participation and the community's feelings of disempowerment are symptoms of the deterioration of these institutions. In the business realm, the current wave of downsizing, layoffs and a collapsing housing and real estate market is a result of unstable institutions. The political community's response is to spend money it doesn't have, exacerbating the decline of business as well as religious and civic institutions.

Why We Need the Institutions More Than Ever Before

Today in Washington, our leaders tell us that we face an economic crisis unlike anything in memory, and that dramatic action is needed. But as Hemingway wrote, "there is a difference between motion and action." What we have seen in Washington is motion, and most of it has been designed to increase government. And this only exacerbates the imbalance among the institutions. As noted previously, if government grows, the other institutions are diminished. This is unhealthy, unnecessary and unwise. We need action that will renew our country by restoring the symmetrical design of the four institutions.

Yes, we face an economic crisis in America. But we face something more profound. We face a philosophical and cultural confusion about what kind of country we are and what kind of people we want to be and it is jeopardizing our role in the world.

Do we want government running entire companies and industries? Is government's now dominant role in the automobile industry and a major insurance company where the U.S. should be at this time in history? Do we want to be a government of the people, as Lincoln said, or a people of the government? These are important questions that go to the heart of who we are and what we can be.

Here is one fact that might surprise you: the 2010 federal budget deficit of $1.3 trillion dollars was more than the entire budget of the United States of America in 1990.

Consider the reminiscences of the late syndicated columnist Robert Novak at the occasion of his 40th year as a Washington reporter. Writing in 1997 about how different Washington was when he went there in 1957, Novak recalled how government actually had a budget surplus, and this was when defense spending comprised 65% of the budget. Pointing out that there was no Medicare, no National Endowment for the Arts, no departments of Education, Energy, or Housing and Urban Development, no "Great Society" anti-poverty apparatus, Novak concluded that while we can argue as to whether America was better off or not in 1957, "it is inarguable that America was freer then."

It goes without saying that a look at the budget of 2009 and the stimulus program of that year is light years removed from the federal government the young Novak first reported on.

Is this what we want for our country and our future? Can we spend our way back to prosperity and greatness?

Yes, we face profound challenges today. But the answers will come not from more money or more programs. The answers will come from restoring the institutions to their proper place and balance in American life.

Restoring the Four Institutions

Thomas Jefferson wrote in the Declaration of Independence: "We hold these truths to be self-evident: that all men are created equal, that they are endowed by their Creator with certain inalienable rights, that among these are life, liberty and the pursuit of happiness: that to secure these rights, governments are instituted among men..." Yet today, more than 200 years after Jefferson's words of liberation and more than 100 years after Kuyper's largely ignored Cultural Mandate, America's institutions are weaker, not stronger. We have lost sight of how the four institutions were designed to work for us.

It's time to rebuild, refocus and rededicate our country to the institutions that will make us great. Furthermore, it's time to apply the institutions of the Cultural Mandate to the challenges we face.

At this critical juncture in the history of the United States and Western civilization in general, in order to right the obvious wrongs, it has become necessary to define the pursuit of happiness. Therefore, in the Pursuit of Happiness, we are endowed by our Creator with:

> The right to a relationship with a higher power
>   and the free exercise of faith
> The right to a loving mother and a protective father
> The right to meaningful and profitable employment
> The right to an orderly and a safe society

We recognize that to secure the Rights of Life, Liberty and the Pursuit of Happiness, the institutions of Faith, Family, Work and Government were established among all men and women.

We can no longer afford the enactment of laws or expenditure of tax dollars in an attempt to meet every social challenge. The classic case in point is the Department of Education. The Cabinet-level department was created in 1979 in large part as a payoff to the National Education Association by President Jimmy Carter. The legislation creating the department was passed by a four-vote margin in the House of Representatives. Over the next 31 years, more than $1 trillion has been spent on improving the quality of American education under the aegis of the Department of Education. But after all these years and all those tax dollars, test scores in college exams for high school students are lower than in 1979, while the high school dropout rate and the rate of illiteracy have risen dramatically nationwide. On a regular basis we are told that America is in danger of falling behind in terms of students mastering needed mathematics and other skills and that (you guessed it!) brand new government programs are needed to remedy this.

One cannot say definitively that this would not be the case if the Department of Education had not been created. But the evidence is strong that creation of the department and its resulting spending has not improved the quality and results of public education in America.

We must replace the Pavlovian response of throwing more money at a problem with a deliberate attempt to define the purpose of each institution and begin to restore each of them.

So, this is the road home: restoring the Four Institutions and bringing with them new understandings of the inalienable rights given to all Americans.

The New World Order is the Old World Order

Beginning with our culture, not government, we can reinforce and strengthen the architecture of our great pyramid. And with it, we can continue building it even higher, creating a more perfect union.

Chapter Three

The Faith Institution

Persuasion

In 1862, a book was released in France that would change the world. The author was Victor Hugo, perhaps the greatest of all French poets. But for seventeen years he had labored quietly on a major novel about human suffering and injustice. When he finished the manuscript and sent it to his publisher, he worried about the reaction. He nervously sent a simple note to his publisher: "?" To which his publisher wrote back: "!"

The book was entitled *Les Miserables* and became an overnight sensation worldwide. And it was on this literary canvass that one of the most beautiful scenes of redemption was created—the story of Jean Valjean and the Bishop.

Jean Valjean is the stranger, recently released from prison and angry at the unjust sentence – serving thirteen years for stealing a loaf of bread to feed his sister's starving family. The Bishop graciously takes the man in and offers him something to eat and a place to stay. Instead of being happy to be free or grateful for having a place to stay, he rages with an intense bitterness at the injustices of his life. Hugo writes that even his soul has "withered." The Bishop senses this and tells him: "You have left a place of suffering. But listen, there will be more joy in heaven over the tears of a repentant sinner, than over the white robes of a hundred good men. If you are leaving that sorrowful place with hate and anger against men, you are worthy of compassion; if you leave it with goodwill, gentleness, and peace, you are better than any of us."

Valjean does not repent. Instead, he returns the Bishop's kindness by stealing his silver and running away into the night. When the police catch him, they bring him back to face the Bishop. Here is how Hugo tells the story:

The Bishop advanced as quickly as his great age permitted. "Ah! Here you are!" He exclaimed, looking at Jean Valjean. "I am glad to see you. Well, but how is this? I gave you the candlesticks too, which are of silver like the rest, and for which you can certainly get two hundred francs. Why did you not carry them away with your forks and spoons?"

Jean Valjean opened his eyes wide, and stared at the venerable Bishop with an expression which no human tongue can render any account of.

"Monseigneur," said the brigadier of gendarmes, "so what this man said is true, then? We came across him. He was walking like a man who is running away. We stopped him to look into the matter. He had this silver—."

"And he told you," interposed the Bishop with a smile, "that it had been given to him by a kind old fellow of a priest with whom he had passed the night? I see how the matter stands. And you have brought him back here? It is a mistake."

"In that case," replied the brigadier, 'we can let him go?"

"Certainly," replied the Bishop.

The gendarmes released Jean Valjean, who recoiled.

"Is it true that I am to be released?" he said, in an almost inarticulate voice, and as though he were talking in his sleep.

"Yes, thou art released; dost thou not understand?" said one of the gendarmes.

"My friend," resumed the Bishop, "before you go, here are your candlesticks. Take them."

He stepped to the chimney-piece, took the two silver candlesticks, and brought them to Jean Valjean......

....Jean Valjean was trembling in every limb. He took the two candlesticks mechanically, and with a bewildered air.

"Now," said the Bishop, "go in peace. By the way, when you return, my friend, it is not necessary to *pass through the garden. You can always enter and depart through the street door. It is never fastened with anything but a latch, either by day or by night."*

Then, turning to the gendarmes:—

"You may retire, gentlemen."

The gendarmes retired.

Jean Valjean was like a man on the point of fainting.

The Bishop drew near to him, and said in a low voice:—

"Do not forget, never forget, that you have promised to use this money in becoming an honest man."

Jean Valjean, who had no recollection of ever having promised anything, remained speechless. The Bishop had emphasized the words when he uttered them. He resumed with solemnity:—

> *"Jean Valjean, my brother, you no longer belong to evil, but to good. It is your soul that I buy from you; I withdraw it from black thoughts and the spirit of perdition, and I give it to God."*

Although *Les Miserables* is historical fiction, Jean Valjean is a vivid portrayal of a man of vice or the victim of injustice, who has experienced the life changing power of love, compassion, and forgiveness, and becomes a man of virtue. He experienced the true power of faith exercised, and this changed his life. The Bishop's act of charity moved Valjean from a life of vice to one of virtue. He became honest and successful and a giving man for the rest of his life. He became strong enough to help others. He became a giver rather than a taker.

The Free Exercise of Religion

The life changing story of Jean Valjean shows that there is more to the First Amendment to the Bill of Rights than the freedom to worship God. Every major religion is composed of how we relate to a higher power and how we relate to each other. The right to the free exercise of all religions has two manifestations: the freedom to worship God and the freedom to love our neighbor as ourselves. Worshiping God and loving your neighbor as ourselves are the two inalienable religious rights we have in America. Loving our neighbors as ourselves is the persuasive element in American society that produces virtue, freedom, prosperity and independence.

Our first amendment covers the right, not only to worship God freely, but to the free exercise of religion, and that should include charity.

And the government of the United States violates that right with state sponsored charity.

The Founding Fathers' great accomplishment in their Declaration was putting the two institutions that have contributed the most to tyranny in civilization, the Church and Government, into perspective and into their proper roles. The environment they created enabled all institutions to flourish according to their purposes. Government was allowed to protect its citizens, and the Church, or Religion, was allowed its role in promoting the worship of God and persuading people, as the Bishop did, to turn from vice to the virtue that was necessary to sustain a free republic. To put it another way, the Founding Fathers knew that freedom must be accompanied by virtue, and virtue was allowed to thrive under a small government that guaranteed the free exercise of religion, because virtue produced charity.

A modern day bishop would be free to exercise his faith, persuade, or otherwise perform charitable acts in much the same way as the Bishop did in *Les Miserables*. It's true that religious persons are free to do that today. But, there is a poison infecting this virtue building institution and it is stifling religions' ability to build independence in America. That poison is government; the charity partner the church took on beginning in the 1930's.

During the Great Depression, the failure of banks, the crash of the market and high unemployment threatened the very existence of the United States. Much like our president today, FDR was willing to try any amount of Government intervention and experimentation to jumpstart our economy. Jonathan Alter said it best in his book *"The Defining Moment"* when he wrote: "...FDR knew he was on the verge of proposing nothing less than a rewriting of the American social contract. Instead of every man being the captain of his own fate, he envisioned the ship of state carrying a safety net. ....He favored what he called 'cradle to grave' coverage, including national health insurance. But he knew that trying to insulate average Americans from the ravages of the market was a long-term process. So, in public, he borrowed a term from the private sector and spoke vaguely of 'social insurance.'"

In a nationwide radio address carried by CBS-Radio on October 13, 1932, New York Governor and Democratic presidential nominee Roosevelt declared that "even in an ideal community where no one is out of work, there would always be the needs of welfare work conducted through the churches, through private charity and by local government— the need for clinics and hospitals and vocational training, the need for the care of the aged, for care of mental cases and for care of the crippled."

FDR went on to say that "[t]he first principle I would lay down is that the primary duty rests on the community, through local and private agencies to take care of the relief of unemployment. But then we come to a situation where there are so many people out of work that local funds are insufficient. It seems that the organized society known as the State comes into the picture at this point. In other words, the obligation of Government is extended to the next higher unit."

In underscoring his own record of public relief as a governor, Roosevelt vowed to "go a step further and say that where the State itself is unable to fulfill this obligation which lies upon it, *it then becomes the positive duty of the Federal Government to step in to help.* [Emphasis added]."

Government intervention may be necessary in a weakened or failed institution, such as the business institution during the Great Depression. In fact, all institutions relate with each other to some degree. Some have called this "sphere sovereignty," where each institution is sovereign according to its purpose, but functionally interacts with other institutions in the normal course of life. An example of interaction between institutions is the debate over abortion; a collision between a family's freedoms and the government's mandate to protect life. In the case of business and government, however, both institutions must return to their proper roles when the weakened institution becomes stronger. Historically, this has not been the case in America, as Ronald Reagan once joked, the nearest thing to eternal life we will see this side of Heaven is a temporary government program.

The trend toward "government programs" accelerated during the Great Depression and the "general welfare" clause of the Constitution has been used as justification for social spending since. Now, after eighty years of ever increasing "social insurance," the "safety net" has become a dragnet, ensnaring millions, robbing them of the fullest expression of their lives and bankrupting the country. With the ever increasing role of government came spending, an enormous national debt and a weakening of the other institutions in America.

One needs to look no further than the leading index of cultural indicators to see how big government's impact on faith and family has been. And where were the leaders of the business institution when the country slid into the mortgage crisis?

Follow The Charity Money

In 2006 Americans spent a total of $1.2 trillion per year on charitable giving. It is evident how little this charity really works to persuade people to virtue, independence and freedom.

The average charitable giving rate among Americans for more than fifty years has been about 1.5-2% of gross income. That represents about $300 billion per year from individuals. Surprisingly, corporations and foundations comprise only about $100 billion per year, one third the figure given by individuals.

The remaining amount of charitable "giving," $800 billion per year, comes from involuntary tax funded government "charity" – social programs such as food stamps, Medicaid, some forms of Medicare, etc. That means less than 33% of all charity in America comes from the individuals whom the Founding Fathers relied on to maintain virtue in a free society. The balance, 66%, goes to government sponsored charity. And $800 billion was twenty five percent of the federal budget during the George Bush years. Therefore, twenty five percent of your taxes go to social charity programs void of the persuasive characteristics the founding fathers knew were vital to self-rule and a free country.

The Ass-Backward Faith Based Initiative

The institution of faith has become so weak and its purpose so confused that it too seeks government funding through the faith-based initiative. The government/faith relationship is contrary to the original purpose of both institutions. Our American sense of compassion has morphed into a government initiative. Although well intentioned, the Faith Based Initiative is a perfect example of an already weakened institution increasing its reliance on government funding instead of relying on voluntary giving.

When he began running for president in 1999, Texas Governor George W. Bush said: "It is not enough for conservatives like me to praise [compassionate] efforts. It is not enough to call for volunteerism. Without more support and resources, both private and public, we are asking them to make bricks without straw." He went on to propose that, as president, he would spend $8 billion during his first year in office to help social service organizations better serve "the least, the last, and the lost." He also proposed that $6 billion would be set aside for new tax incentives that would generate billions more in private charitable giving. But he didn't stop there. He also promised an additional $1.7 billion a year to fund faith-based (and non-faith-based) groups caring for drug addicts, at-risk youth, and teen moms. And $200 million more would go to create a "Compassion Capital Fund" that would assist and expand successful local programs.

Many on the political right praised this effort as a bold new conservative approach to charity in America. It was anything but that. Bold for sure, but not conservative. Bush only added to what LBJ started with the decisive intervention of government into charity. Government would be involved in funding all kinds of charity programs from drug rehabilitation to poverty. It may have been well-intentioned, but it was ill-conceived.

Why did President Bush think that an organization that can't deliver the mail on time would be able to alleviate drugs or poverty? Government is simply not designed to do such a thing. In retrospect, the Bush approach was completely backward. Instead of making government funds available to faith-based organizations, he should have advocated for a return of charity to the private sector with corresponding budget cuts in social programs. One who understood the truth of this alternative approach was a lady who had given up much to devote her life to genuine private charity.

Mary Lyman Jackson had been a concert pianist, professional model, the widow of an Episcopal pastor, and a mother of three. Following her husband's death, Mrs. Jackson continued his work as chief operating officer of the Exodus House, a shelter in Washington DC's notorious "hood" neighborhood known as Anacostia. In taking on the chore of administering Exodus relief program as well as ministering to the spiritual needs of those who came to her, Mrs. Jackson made one non-negotiable demand of her board of directors: Exodus would never accept federal funds in any form.

"Submitting Exodus to the maw of federal forms and regulations would be both time-consuming and an open door to interfering with the message we were bringing to those who came to the shelter—the word of Jesus Christ," recalled Mrs. Jackson in 2001, after nearly a decade of keeping the doors of Exodus open through small donations and a few major gifts from businesses. "It just wasn't worth it in the long run to accept tax dollars, no matter how much easier it would have made the job of administering Exodus."

Rather than expand government's role in charity, President Bush should have reduced it. He should have looked for ways to encourage more personal charity, rather than funding programs that government bureaucrats liked. The minute the government starts funding a program, the independence, effectiveness, and power of the program is lost. No government program can ever match the power of private charity. And no president should ever try to make it so again. Yet amazingly, President Obama has praised the faith-based initiative and pledged to expand it even more.

Not Off The Hook

The Jean Valjeans of today lobby the federal government for increased social spending on the poor, even though Valjean himself was saved by a bishop. And the Bishop discourages an increase in charitable giving, because government funding to religious organizations may be reduced as a result.

Public Enemy Number One of the restoration of the faith institution is state-sponsored charity. If the institution of faith is to be valid in American society, it must be allowed to persuade to virtue and charity. Government "charity" prevents this free exercise of religion.

Charity has been outsourced. The institution that should be providing charity; caring for the widow and the orphan - individuals, churches, non-profits, etc. - have farmed out at least 66% of the job to the institution of government, which cannot change lives and at best, can only maintain a status quo of dependency. The results of this out-sourcing have been disastrous. Not only is government charity inefficient, it's ineffective in building virtue, in putting people on a path to freedom, independence and prosperity.

Can you imagine a government employee reaching into the bitter, hurt, stone cold heart of Jean Valjean and saying, "my brother, you no longer belong to evil, but to good. It is your soul that I buy from you. I withdraw it from the black thoughts and the spirit of perdition, and I give it to God?"

Government should not be in the charity business. If we must render unto Caesar what is Caesar's for charitable purposes at all, it must be for a very small safety net, not to subvert the virtue building that must occur in the faith institution if freedom is to survive in America.

We must confront the corrosive influence that government programs have had on the Faith Institution. We must acknowledge that government violates the free exercise of religion clause of the First Amendment through government welfare programs.

Where Democratic President Barack Obama wants to expand the government hand in charity beyond the faith-based concept, another Democratic president had a different attitude—and one that resonates to this day.

"The friendliness and charity our countrymen can always be relied upon to relieve their fellow citizens in misfortune," said President Grover Cleveland, "... Federal aid in such cases encourages the expectation of paternal care on the part of the government and weakens the sturdiness of our national character, while it prevents the indulgence among our people of that kindly sentiment and conduct which strengthens the bonds of a common brotherhood."

Even though 25 cents of every tax dollar goes to charity, it does not count toward our moral obligation to love thy neighbor as ourselves. It will not be credited to us. What is levied is not freely given and charity that builds virtue in America must be freely given. For people of conscience, this is a moral imperative that is not subordinate to government.

The time has come to seriously reconsider the intrusion of government into the Faith Institution. We also must reconsider the imperatives that lie at the heart of the Faith Institution: loving our neighbor as ourselves; caring for the widow and the orphan; laying down our lives for one another. These religious principles, which make us a better people and a better nation, are needed again in America.

That's why it's more important than ever to restore the Faith Institution to its rightful place in our national life.

Chapter Four

Institution of Family

Preparation

Jeff Reed came from a very dysfunctional family, and was heading down the wrong path. But he realized that path led to a dead end. So he came up with a solution: he borrowed another family. Usually, parents adopt the child. But Jeff sort of adopted these parents. He began spending time at their house, learning from them, becoming like them. It worked. Today, Jeff is a productive member of society.

Most troubled kids aren't as fortunate. But the point still stands: the impact of a good mom and dad can be tremendous. Years ago, Henry Adams wrote that a "teacher affects eternity; he can never tell where his influence stops." The ultimate teacher is the parent. And parents have the ability to impact eternity by shaping the lives of their children.

And Jeff Reed was right about something very important: he was entitled to a mother and a father. All children are entitled to this.

Seth Ireland wasn't as fortunate as Jeff Reed.

As a 10 year-old growing up in Fresno, California, he became acquainted with pain and suffering. But unlike most of us, he couldn't escape the pain by going home; home was where the pain was waiting for him. His father once beat him so badly with a belt that Child Protective Services stepped in. When Seth's mother got a new boyfriend, things got worse, not better. Neighbors reported hearing screams from inside the house. But no one who really could, helped.

On December 29, 2008, Seth's mother stood and watched as her boyfriend kicked, punched and even stomped on Seth's head with his size 13 feet. The battered and beaten little boy collapsed into a coma and later died at the hospital.

The sad fact is that Seth Ireland never had a chance. Inside his home, he found himself on a battlefield as unstable adults often attacked him. Outside his home, the local government did almost nothing to help him despite repeated warnings something was wrong.

Between August and December, the local police were called to Seth's house 12 times, usually after a neighbor reported hearing screaming next door. Yet Seth's mother's boyfriend, LeBaron Vaughn, was never arrested until he was charged with Seth's murder.

Local Child Protective Services knew what was going on. A couple of months before Seth's murder, a caseworker investigated and found that there was "possible physical and emotional abuse [and] neglect" in the home. Yet later, when a neighbor reported hearing violence, a caseworker declined to remove Seth from the home, writing in a report that "the allegations appeared to be unfounded and that the kids deny any abuse or neglect."

Seth Ireland never had a chance. He was failed by everyone. His family killed him and his government was unable to save him.

But his death need not be in vain. His story points to an obvious truth: every child is entitled to a loving mother and father. Not abusive tyrants who are parents in name only, but real moms and dads who love and care for them, and properly raise them.

Some may argue that government programs can take the place of parents, that "professionals" know better, but the story of Seth Ireland reminds us that government not only can't do the jobs of parents, it can rarely do anything to save children in a bad home. The sacredness of the family institution, and the parental rights associated with it, precludes any agency or institution from being an adequate substitute for a loving family.

Seth Ireland never had a chance. We can make sure every other kid does.

How the Family Prepares Kids

Fred Bigler knows the importance of families. For years, he served as a probation officer in juvenile corrections in Modesto, California. He saw young people headed down the wrong path early in life, with hardened hearts, closed minds and limited futures. All these children were different, but in one sense they were all the same. A common theme often ran through their biographies: they were the products of broken homes.

Rather than an institution, we too often refer to the family as a moral or religious "issue" in our political and cultural discourse. But the family institution has a unique role to play in America: it prepares future Americans. It teaches and shapes them. So if the family isn't working the way it should, the country suffers.

The breakdown of the family is the reason that people like Fred Bigler are so busy. "It's heartbreaking to see these kids committing crimes and heading to jail because they came from a home that gave them no hope and no love," he laments. Fred recalls one young man in particular who came from a broken home and then went straight from juvenile detention to the streets and back to the prisons. Eventually, he used and sold drugs. And he never was able to piece his life back together again. "It was a shame but he never had a chance," Fred concluded.

The only chance any child ever gets is being in a functional two-parent family. This is where the child's journey begins. Without it, it becomes almost impossible to get on and stay on track.

Writing in her book *Save the Males*, Pulitzer Prize-winning columnist Kathleen Parker observed that "[t]he gradual eradication of fathers from children's lives—often in the service of feminist goals that seemed like a good idea at the time—has been our most dubious achievement. Thanks to divorce, unwed motherhood, and policies that unfairly penalize and marginalize fathers, 30 to 40 per cent of all American children sleep in a home where their father doesn't. Although most women who marry and have children don't intend to divorce and become single parents, single motherhood by choice is becoming increasingly popular as unmarried celebrities are applauded for accessorizing with designer babies."

"Indeed," Parker concludes, "growing up without a father is the most reliable predictor of poverty and all the familiar social pathologies affecting children, including drug abuse, truancy, delinquency, and sexual promiscuity."

Fred Bigler is now the Director of Community Support Services for the Stanislaus County Office of Education. From this position he sees the family institution as vital to all aspects of society. A family that produces a well-rounded child helps all of society because that child will be productive, law-abiding and patriotic. On the other hand, a family that produces a dysfunctional child is a costly burden to society because the odds increase he will be unemployed, commit crime, be incarcerated and otherwise drain social service funds.

The family has an enormous impact on the development of the individual and society.

People often wonder how they can make a difference. We may not have the capacity to love 30,000 people in a baseball stadium, but we do have that capacity in the small circle of family. The family institution is unique among the four institutions in that it directly affects the development of a person from the very beginning of life. It is the cradle where life begins and no institution can replicate the critical work that must take place in this institution.

Research has shown that the first years of life are vitally important to the success of a person and his impact on society. If certain needs are not met in the beginning, there is little chance that positive character traits will ever be developed. The individual is robbed of their best chance of success and society is the worse for it.

The impact of family breakdown can be clearly seen in the following statistics. From 1960 to 1990 there has been a:

560% increase in violent crime

419% increase in illegitimate births

400% increase in divorce

300% increase in single parent families

200% increase in teenage suicides

Kishora Mabubani, Far Eastern Economic Review

From a societal point of view, the institution of Family is less about relationships and more about strong bonds that prepare the next generation. A successful family produces competent, capable people who are more likely to live independent of social services; a result that is more beneficial to society and less costly to government. The family institution is crucial to the success of America. Another institution cannot replicate the role of the family.

"As important as stable families are to the goal of raising well-adjusted children with character, self-discipline, and purpose," wrote Kathleen Parker in *Save the Males*, "families serve yet another function: They keep government in its place. This is not a small point, if one we seldom hear about. When we weaken the family unit, we become vulnerable to other forces. Incrementally, government fills the void once occupied by parents. Social services feed, house, and clothe the children of destroyed families, while the Department of Education instructs proper ways of thinking about moral issues. As long as everyone is feeling good, getting their instant gratification at the trough of fast food and free porn, one hardly notices that autonomy is being surrendered to external authorities."

If we measure the strength of the family institution in terms of the needs of a child being met, then the American family is disintegrating rapidly. And while single parents, grandparents and loving communities do their best to stand in the gap, a child's best chance in life is, and will always be, with a two parent, Mother and Father, nuclear family. We can debate all we want about what defines a marriage, but a loving, devoted Mother and Father will always define what is best for a child.

Family and the Individual

"There is a very clear series of developmental stages that every child goes through," Fred Bigler says, drawing on years of research and experience in youth programs. "And only the family can properly deal with each stage."

The first stage occurs from the time a child is born to the time he/she reaches age 2. This is when the child needs one thing above all else: love. Being new in the world, a baby needs to feel the safety and security that comes from love, which can be expressed in many ways. It comes from words, yes. But mostly, it comes from actions: a touch, a smile. There is a tradition in Bali that a child is never to touch the ground until the age of 2, constantly held and cared for. This is how a baby that is still learning to talk knows that he or she is loved. What other entity can meet this need? What other program can touch or hold a child and say "I love you" to him or her? Only the family can. Only a mother and father can do this. This is the developmental stage when children trust in their parents' love and develop a sense of peace. The character flaw of fear, which leads to personal insecurities and social withdrawal, is best corrected during the first two years when an infant bonds with loving parents. A properly loved child will trust in his parents' love, resulting in peace and security.

The second stage occurs during the ages 3-6. This is the disciplinary stage. By discipline, this means not just punishment, which is the most negative form, but softer discipline, which is covered in love. In these early childhood years, parental figures challenge the child to receive direction, obey and follow the rules. When children refuse to submit, they become unstable. Our prisons today are filled with people who never learned to obey or follow the rules at this early stage. When they submit, they gain a sense of acceptance. When children submit to parental will, their self-will is kept from transforming into anger and instability. But the key is the sequencing. "The discipline comes after the love is first established," Bigler says. "A child that is loved is a child that will submit to discipline."

The third developmental stage is training. This occurs somewhere around ages 7-9. This is when the child begins to learn. And who are the first teachers? Parents, of course. Parents read books to the child, teach words to the child. At about age 7, the mind is ready to begin fully absorbing these lessons. Teachers and schools have a big role to play in the training stage as well. But parents are the first teachers. In addition, this is the stage where kids learn socialization skills and begin to successfully interact with other kids. This is when Little League begins and Sunday School starts. But the foundation is laid in the home. When children receive parental training, their natural self-deceit is kept from evolving into anti-social behavior. A child that has been loved and disciplined at home is a child that is ready to be trained and ready to interact with others.

The fourth developmental stage is protection. As the child approaches the teen years, he or she is vulnerable to outside influences. It's a parent's job to protect the child from sexual abuse, drug dependency and violence in this very dangerous world. And children have a natural desire for self-gratification. When children are protected from temptations by their parents, they are protected from possible harm. Children need the firm hand of a parent to keep them safe.

The fifth and final developmental stage is identity. This occurs in the teen years when kids try to figure out who they are and what they believe. And a child is more likely to reach a satisfactory identity if he or she has come from a home where they were nurtured with love, discipline, training and protection. These children honor their mother and father, learn to work, maintain a clear conscience before God and obey the laws of the land. When children submit and serve others, their selfishness is checked and they are allowed to form a positive identity. All kids need a sense of worth. And that sense starts in the home.

"Only the family can meet the needs of children at all five stages," Bigler concludes. No government spending, no federal program can ever match the loving touch of a family. Nor should it try to. This is the family's job. And the only issue is how best to restore the family so that it can do its job well.

What happens when families don't meet the needs of kids at the five developmental stages? We all pay the price.

With the increasing number of broken families in America, it's not difficult to imagine the impact on the children and on society. Sadly, we don't have to imagine the impact; we can look at the empirical research that has been done on the subject. As a general principle, research shows that a broken family can lead to poverty.

A Heritage Foundation report found that an "analysis of the social science literature demonstrates that the root cause of poverty and income disparity is linked undeniably to the presence or absence of marriage. Broken families earn less and experience lower levels of educational achievement. Worse, they pass the prospect of meager incomes and family instability on to their children, ensuring a continuing if not expanding cycle of economic distress."

In particular, the report found: "Of families with children in the lowest quintile of earnings, 73 percent are headed by single parents; 95 percent in the top quintile are headed by married couples." Simply put, a broken family leads to poverty; a two-parent family leads to prosperity.

Also, the research shows that broken families lead to other social pathologies: "The children of divorced parents are more likely to get pregnant and give birth outside of marriage, especially if the divorce occurred during their mid-teenage years, and twice as likely to cohabit as are children of married parents. Moreover, divorce appears to result in a reduction of the educational accomplishments of the affected children, weakens their psychological and physical health, and predisposes them to rapid initiation of sexual relationships and higher levels of marital instability. It also raises the probability that they will never marry, especially for boys."

It is clear that broken families lead to poverty, more broken families, more unwed pregnancies, more cohabitation, reduced educational achievement and health.

Imagine for a moment how much better society would be if the institution of the family was restored. According to the research, we would have more prosperity, fewer broken marriages, fewer unwed pregnancies, less cohabitation, greater educational achievement and increased health. Imagine how great America would become if cultural indicators like divorce rates, teen pregnancies and domestic violence actually decreased instead of increased. Now that is a real stimulus plan!

A functional two-parent family for every child is no longer an option; it's a necessity. It's the only way to reverse these pathologies and create a better America.

In 1920, G.K. Chesterton may have summarized the case that the family makes for a free society and thus a better society: "The ideal for which [family] stands in the state is liberty. It stands for liberty for the very simple reason. . . [that] it is the only . . [institution] that is at once necessary and voluntary. It is the only check on the state that is bound to renew itself as eternally as the state, and more naturally than the state. . . This is the only way in which truth can ever find refuge from public persecution, and the good man survives the bad government."

Family and Society

Art Rolnick is not a revolutionary; he's an economist. Since 1985, he has crunched numbers at the Federal Reserve Bank of Minneapolis. "We make money the old fashioned way," he often jokes, "we print it."

A few years ago, he became interested in how local communities and states spend big money to create economic development. As a conservative, he worried about the effectiveness of this. As a lifelong Minnesotan, he wondered if that money couldn't be better spent.

And so he began studying the problem. "Conventional economic development policies use public subsidies and tax breaks to attract businesses and jobs from one location to another," he says. "Such polices lead to economic bidding wars and are counterproductive. Allowing cities and states to lure businesses from other cities and states with public funds only moves jobs around; it does not create any new ones." In particular, Rolnick became convinced that taxpayer-funded sports stadiums were uneconomical and he became a leading critic. But he's careful to point out that government-funded stadiums are a symptom of the larger problem—government subsidies do not create economic growth. "If providing public subsidies to private businesses are the wrong way to promote economic development, what is the right way?" he began to ask a few years ago. And like the scholar he is, he began to research the issue. "The research on this question is quite persuasive. It shows that state and local governments should instead use limited resources on developing their public goods and, in particular, their communities' human capital, which is their workforce."

It's not often that an economist at the Federal Reserve talks about investing in people, rather than companies or markets. But Rolnick was convinced this was the only investment that would return a dividend. Not long after he came to this realization, Rolnick attended an event for the "Ready 4 K" program that supports early education. During a discussion at the event, two officials were arguing for more state funding. "I naively raised my hand and said, 'This sounds good, but I can make all kinds of moral arguments for K–12, higher education, reducing pollution, reducing crime,'" he remembers. "'I just think you're not going to make much headway without making the economic case for it.'"

An economic case for early childhood education? The hosts of the event were so startled by the suggestion that they recommended Rolnick research it and get back to them. Perhaps they thought he would find no evidence for his argument.

But Rolnick did research it and he did find the evidence. He co-authored a report called "Early Childhood Development: Economic Development with a High Public Return." Maybe for the first time ever, a serious academic case was made for early childhood programs with strong parental involvement, as an economic incentive. Rolnick's report mentioned his previous work on government subsidies of business and how no one wins. Just because a company gets tax abatement and leaves one city for another, the country as a whole is not creating new jobs, it's just re-locating them.

On the other hand, Rolnick's report argued that a great return would come to cities and the country with an increased investment in children.

To prove it, the report cited a study of 3 and 4 year olds, that began in 1962 in Ypsilanti, Michigan. Half the children received intensive early education services. The others didn't. Years later, when they reached age 27, they were interviewed. Some 65 percent of the early education students graduated from high school; only 45 percent of those without early education graduated. Further studies revealed that assistance from ages 0 – 4 with intense parental involvement produced even better results. Moreover, the early education students earned more money professionally and were less likely to end up in jail.

The report decided that early education was vitally important and that it could produce a 16 percent annual rate of return on initial investments. Thus, Art Rolnick the economist became Art Rolnick the revolutionary. He urged the creation in Minnesota of a $1.5 billion state endowment to permanently fund early education for all 3 to 4 year-olds from low-income homes in the state. After all, Rolnick believes a life well-lived costs society less.

But ultimately, Rolnick believes the issue comes down to the family. "What are we doing?" he asks. "We're empowering people to be better parents and giving them resources to do things that middle-class parents already do."

Art Rolnick is asking the right questions even if some of his answers are wrong. The answer is not another government spending program on education. If we realize true freedom is the ability to live life in the Face of God, that loving our neighbor as ourselves is a function of faith, then we cannot rely on the government as the second best solution. The answer is more private charity directed to the inalienable rights of children to a caring father and mother. This will be more effective and more powerful than anything the government could do.

It's been said that while most people spend their lives building careers, parents spend their careers building lives...the lives of the loved ones in their homes. Today in America, we need to empower parents once again. We need to embolden families once again. We need to restore the Institution of the Family.

Rolnick's thesis is simple, but profound: a life well lived costs society less than a life poorly lived. His argument for investing in early childhood programs is not one based on good intentions, but on solid research. He knows that the only thing more expensive than investing in an at-risk child is not investing in one.

Children have an inalienable right to a functional mother and a father. No government, religion or business will ever supplant this right. In fact, government does not honor or respect this institution as it should. And the time has come to redeem that right, for all children, once and for all. Steps need to be taken to ensure that this right is protected and preserved. Every child deserves a mother and a father. The stakes are high...the time is now.

The alternative can most succinctly be characterized by a central plank written by Karl Marx and Friedrich Engels in *The Communist Manifesto*: "Abolition of the family!"

Chapter Five

The Institution of Work

Provision

In 1941, Hollywood released a movie that many consider to be the greatest film of all time. "Citizen Kane" starred Orson Welles as newspaper tycoon Charles Foster Kane, whose business success and vast political influence had still left him personally unsatisfied. After Kane dies, a reporter is intrigued by his last word: "Rosebud." The reporter begins an investigation into the man's life. He discovers a remarkable rise to power, wealth and fame. As a child, Kane had been torn away from his family. But once he entered the newspaper business, he achieved incredible success.

Eventually, he married the niece of the President of the United States and built a huge estate that he called "Xanadu." Inside the estate, he collected extravagant art and other treasures and seemed to have it all. But appearances are deceiving. Married and then divorced, he neglected his second wife who eventually also sought a divorce. He became increasingly isolated and eccentric. At his death, he was alone and depressed. He had gained the world, but lost his soul.

The reporter never discovers the meaning of the word, "Rosebud." But in the movie's last scene, the audience is shown a fire where relics from the Xanadu mansion are being destroyed now that Kane has died. One of them is his cherished childhood sled. On the sled is painted the word "Rosebud." In Kane's last moments on earth, he didn't think about his business empire or his professional achievements. He thought about his lost childhood and the simpler things of life. Perhaps, the sled is a token of the only time in his life when he was poor. Perhaps, more than this, it represents the only time in his life when he was truly happy and wanted for nothing, a period in his life uncorrupted by money.

Part of what made the movie such a success was that it was widely believed to have been a fictional account of a man familiar to Americans of that time: William Randolph Hearst. Hearst was a powerful newspaper publisher who wanted it all. Perhaps his most notorious act was his role in using his news empire to help create a war. He saw the

Cuban Revolution of 1895 as a business opportunity. He invested huge amounts of resources into supporting Cuba Librè, the Cuban insurgent forces. He also made a point of reporting negatively on Spain. The goal was to sell papers and make money.

When the *U.S.S. Maine* mysteriously exploded in Havana Harbor, Hearst immediately began stoking the fires of war. His newspaper's reporting is believed to have helped create public pressure for war with Spain. Once the fighting started, he personally went to Cuba along with his reporters. According to the legend, James Creelman, a Hearst reporter, led an assault on a Spanish blockhouse and was wounded. When Hearst found him, he allegedly pronounced: "I'm sorry you're hurt. But wasn't it a splendid fight? We beat every paper in the world!" This was Hearst in a nutshell: oblivious to the distinction between reporting and fighting a war and concerned only with the bottom line.

Not surprisingly, Hearst was outraged when he heard about the making of "Citizen Kane" and worked tirelessly to try to stop the movie. He hoped to prevent the release of the film altogether. Unsuccessful in this effort, he then pressured movie theaters to not show it. Given his enormous clout, many acceded to his request resulting in less-than-spectacular numbers at the box office. Yet the movie endured and today is considered a classic. The movie has survived for nearly 70 years in part, because it speaks a truth known to all Americans: that there is a price to be paid by the individual and society, when we have the wrong emphasis on business. Work is a vital part of life. But it is just that: a part of life. If it becomes all-consuming then someone pays a price—society, our spouses, our children, ourselves.

A true-to-life example of emptiness in a life of power and riches is that of Walter Winchell, one of the early architects of the gossip column. As his biographer Neal Gabler wrote: "By one estimate, fifty million Americans—out of an adult population of roughly seventy-five million—either listened to his weekly radio broadcast or read his daily column, which, at its height in the late thirties and forties, was syndicated in more than two thousand newspapers; it was according to one observer, 'the largest continuous audience ever possessed by a man who was neither politician nor divine.'"

Winchell was courted by politicians and at least two presidents, had hit songs written about him and his column, and was featured in two films that became box office hits. But eventually Winchell's column lost its flagship, the *Daily Mirror*, following the strike that finished the New York paper in the early 1960's. The most-listened to radio broadcaster could not make the transition to the new medium of television in the 1950's. The image of him that would stick was not that of the plucky populist columnist but that of a mean-spirited and self-absorbed megalomaniac, much like "J.J. Hunsecker," the gossip columnist portrayed by Burt Lancaster in the film *Sweet Smell of Success* who is assumed to be based on Winchell. As Gabler wrote, "After a Dickensian childhood, vaudeville and tabloids, divorce, tragedy, suicides, betrayals, threats, and mental illness, . .Winchell's life became a paradigm of what one might call the tragedy of celebrity. He lived by fame and died by neglect.. . And when the show finally ended its run, he was left in costume with no role to play and nothing inside himself upon which to draw."

When Winchell died in 1972, less than 150 people attended his funeral in New York. As biographer Gabler put, "In the end, few remembered, and fewer cared."

In the end, Kane had wasted his life pursuing riches that were left behind. Ahead of him was the grave and the realization that none of this, not even the clothes on his back, was going with him. And all he could think about at the end was the simpler time of his childhood when life was more balanced.

Winchell spent his lifetime burnishing his name on the public consciousness and did so at the expense of personal happiness: he spent much of his life apart from wife June, daughter Walda went through a tumultuous personal life, and son Walter, Jr. committed suicide. When his professional career had faded, Winchell had little on the personal front to comfort him.

Sometimes in the *busyness* of living we lose sight of the *business* of life.

Recent scandals on Wall Street have reminded us all of what happens when the focus is on nothing but money. The purpose of the institution of work is provision. In its proper context it has the potential to generate wealth for all.

Business and the Individual

Who is responsible for the 2008 market crash? The individual is, according to Nobel laureate Joseph E. Stiglitz. He wrote an economic analysis for *Vanity Fair* entitled "Wall Street's Toxic Message." He makes the case that, in this current crisis, the reputation of American-style capitalism will have taken a beating and disillusioned developing nations may well turn their back on the free market, posing new threats to global stability and U.S. security. He described the Four Horsemen of the Wall Street Apocalypse as Mendacity, Stupidity, Greed and Arrogance. All of this describes the actions of certain individual entrepreneurs on Wall Street.

Mendacity, Stupidity, Greed and Arrogance led us into the Great Depression and into our current economic mess. And as it opened the door to government intervention in the 1930's, it has done again today. The social ideas that sprang forth from communism and fascism then are alive and thriving today. They sit in stark contrast to America's role in the world – the vanguard of freedom to live life in the face of God through four institutions, each meeting a basic need in all of us.

What we do in business as Americans has a profound affect. When the institution is strong, great things can happen. But when it is tainted by the Four Horsemen, the door swings open for government to intervene, providing social planners the opportunity to rob us of freedom and eventually destroy the other God given institutions. Put another way, one can spoil it for all.

Certainly, the recent suit against Goldman-Sachs by the Securities and Exchange Commission and the resulting nationally-televised probe into the Wall Street colossus put human faces on the Four Horsemen—or at least on one of them.

In April, Goldman Sachs trader Fabrice Tourre testified before the Senate about his role in crafting "Abacus 2007." This was the focus of the controversy surrounding Goldman Sachs. It involved a portfolio of mortgage instruments through which Wall Street tycoon John Poulsen made more than $1 billion during the housing collapse of 2007 and investors (whom the SEC alleges were misled about the status of the instruments) suffered losses. The 31-year-old Tourre offered no regrets in his testimony, except for the language in his now-public e-mails in which he nicknamed himself "Fabulous Fab" and vowed to be the "only potential survivor. . .standing in the middle of all of these complex, highly-leveraged exotic trades."

"He's the real-life Gordon Gekko from the movie *Wall Street,*" concluded *Newsweek* days after Tourre's testimony. He's a doppelgänger to Michael Lewis's autobiographical protagonist in *Liar's Poker,* who sells bad products to unknowing chump investors, and he's becoming a cultural icon to his contemporaries because they empathize with him. One of them could just as easily have been the salesman on the Abacus deal, if only they had been that smart or lucky.

"There's a self-serving role in this. If what he did is wrong, then what they do is wrong on a daily basis," says Adam Galinsky, professor of ethics and leadership at Northwestern University's Kellogg School of Management. "It's not wrong to them, because it's the water they swim in.'"

One of the more poignant ironies of contemporary timing was that less than two weeks after the world got a glimpse of and began its fascination with "Fabulous Fab," producer Oliver Stone premiered his sequel to *Wall Street*, with Michael Douglas reprising his role as Gordon Gekko 27 years later, the sequel added a new character—Gekko's son-in-law, now on the fast track himself on Wall Street.

In a perfect world—men and women are free to enjoy life; free to pursue happiness in the face of God. Each life on earth has a purpose and our purpose is found in fellowship with God, creating families and working. Our purpose shows itself in the desires of the heart and manifests itself through these directives. In our work we build the other institutions.

Each of us is given four institutions in which to pursue happiness.

In his book, *Wild at Heart*, John Eldredge writes about the instinct to succeed that is planted by God inside of each person. "God meant something when we were created and if we are ever to find ourselves, we must find what he has set in the heart. What if those deep desires in our hearts are telling us is the truth, revealing to us the life we were meant to live? God gave us eyes so that we might see; he gave us ears that we might hear; he gave us wills that we might choose, and he gave us hearts that we might live. The way we handle our hearts means everything." He continues: "What about the over achievers, the men running hard at life, blindly pressing their way ahead? Their casualties are usually their marriages, their families, their health and their faith."

Rick Warren makes the same point. In his book, *A Purpose-Driven Life*, the popular pastor writes about the vocational calling each of us has. Although a career should be extremely rewarding when kept in perspective, he warns that what we do professionally isn't about us, it's about God. "Life is about letting God use you for his purposes, not using him for your own purpose," says Pastor Warren.

Think back to the fictional Charles Foster Kane and the real-life Walter Winchell. Their lives were unbalanced because they over-emphasized business and celebrity. And the other areas of their lives suffered as a result. In the end, Kane's pursuit of business left him so empty that he yearned for a time in his life when he was poor, had only his mother, and was truly happy. Winchell's pursuit of celebrity and influence left him even a more pitiable figure because he had neither, nor did he the love of close family members with which to fall back upon.

The institution of business is for the generation of wealth. But what is done with the wealth and the pursuit of it can do even more harm to people than any other institution. An inspiration to take on risk, develop a product and sell it is unique and rewarding. When a family is sacrificed in its attainment, when a soul is lost and, when laws are broken in its attainment, it is wrong. When the all-out pursuit of Mammon—that is, the false good, avarice, and worldly gain— sacrifices our families and our relationship with God, it is wrong.

More than any other institution, business has the ability to distract people and unbalance their lives. And yet too often individuals pursue business with the wrong motive— sacrificing their principles along the way. In pursuit of the Mammon, they lose sight of the Golden Rule. And in the end, they lose both money and honor. Brevity enters the picture and stays until the bitter end. They drop the ball when they realize, in the end, that none of what was pursued can be taken to the next world. Then they themselves cry, "Rosebud."

Business and Society

It is interesting that the growth of government and the decline in the four institutions began in earnest during the collapse of the economy and the subsequent Great Depression. The business cycle always has had its highs and lows, but the Great Depression was the lowest of them all. It hit when the world was brimming with new humanistic world views like fascism and communism. The ideas of Karl Marx and Darwinism had their greatest influence on the 20th century. The failure of business created a perfect opportunity for social experimentation, and FDR was ready to experiment.

One fascinating "prequel" to the Roosevelt presidency and the New Deal was the motion picture *Gabriel Over the White House*, filmed and released in 1932 and released in theatres before President-elect Roosevelt took office the following March. In the film, Walter Huston plays a political hack and ladies' man who is elected president during the Depression. Injured in an automobile accident, the new President is visited by the Archangel Gabriel and recovers quickly. He promptly declares martial law, and rules as a benign dictator: the Depression is met with widespread public works projects; he dispatches the Army to round up gangsters, who are promptly tried before secret tribunals and executed; and he makes a plea to fellow world leaders to pay back their debts from the World War and end war as a means of settling disputes.

Jonathan Alter and most modern historians of the New Deal cite *Gabriel Over the White House* as an influence on the course FDR was about to take. By all accounts, the President saw the movie as many as five times and invited starring actor Huston to the White House for cocktails.

The Depression and the New Deal have been studied and restudied, and argued about, but what began during that era had a great effect on the institutions of the Cultural Mandate. And the impact on all of society has been tremendous.

Because we have let business dominate our lives, we have abdicated charity to government. Because we have let business dominate our lives, the rest of the world views America, not as a shining city on a hill as it once was, but as a decadent place of soulless materialism.

Several years ago, a well-respected man in New York established a lucrative hedge fund known as Ascot Partners.

Many of New York's most affluent people invested in the fund. Year after year, the Ascot Partners fund delivered good returns for the investors. Too good, it turned out. When the stock market collapsed in September 2008, many of these investors came to collect their money. But there was none to collect.

The fund had been a "Ponzi scheme" for years—it would take today's investors' money to pay yesterday's investors. No one was actually making any money except for the founder, Bernie Madoff.

When he pled guilty to all charges in 2009, Madoff tried to explain how a businessman in search of a legitimate product got so off track. He explicitly admitted that his fund was a Ponzi scheme, but said it hadn't started out that way. He said that during the recession of the early 1990's, he began the fraud believing it would be a temporary measure until the economy improved. But the money and the temptation were too great. He could not let go of the scheme. "As the years went by, I realized my risk, and this day would inevitably come," he confessed, "I cannot adequately express how sorry I am for my crimes."

Bernie Madoff didn't set out to be a crook; he set out to be a businessman. He was a classic cynic: he knew the cost of everything and the value of nothing. And so for a few pieces of silver he gave away his soul and destroyed the lives and savings of countless people.

This is what happens when the business institution becomes distorted, and when it becomes an obsession. This is what happens when we have prosperity without a purpose.

In the 1920's America experienced a similar time to our own: great economic growth followed by a dramatic collapse of the economy. F. Scott Fitzgerald made this period famous with his book *The Great Gatsby*, in which the title character is a mysterious man who seems to have it all, even though no one knows much about him or his business.

When people seek money and fame at all costs, everyone pays the bill. Just like the stock market crash in 1929, the 2008-09 collapse was brought about by people who forgot that even in business, the best way to do well is to do good. In our current era, Bernie Madoff played the perfect Great Gatsby, creating a fictional wealth that eventually was exposed and many people were hurt in the process.

The unethical loan shark encouraging people into homes they could not afford in order to make a fast buck and the politician practicing social engineering and appropriating money America doesn't have are just two examples of how society is out of balance. And that makes the American future uncertain. It damages us both at home and abroad. Our financial weakness makes the world a more dangerous place. Too much time worshiping at the altar of materialism changes the world's view of America.

In the 1800s, Frenchman Alexis de Tocqueville toured the United States and coined the phrase "American Exceptionalism" to describe the unique role America played in the world. He wrote: "The position of the Americans is therefore quite exceptional, and it may be believed that no democratic people will ever be placed in a similar one." He was right; it was a dramatic leap forward in freedom – the freedom to live life in fellowship with God through four strong institutions functioning according to their purpose.

But the dramatic failures in the business institution during the Stock Market Crash of 1929 opened the door to government growth and the decline of the other institutions. It opened the door to leaders who practiced social experimentation on a confused society. And today, with decades of socialism devastating the other institutions, the American Exceptionalism described by de Tocqueville has been significantly compromised.

The New World Order is the Old World Order

In America, we need to restore the concept that individuals have the *right* to pursue a vocation, but they have the *responsibility* to do it honestly and honorably.

How much is enough? When the American people are bombarded with new products and things that promise, in terms of the heart, what they can never deliver, we end up a society of debtors, and holders of things with no real value.

We need to turn away from Madoff and look again for Rosebud.

It's time to restore the Institution of business in America. Honest work must be held in honor again.

Chapter Six

The Institution of Government

Protection

In the 1932 presidential election, Franklin Roosevelt campaigned on a promise to create a "New Deal" for the American worker. He was less specific about what that meant. But in March 1933, he took office and launched an aggressive program to use the government to help create jobs and wealth.

Many Americans believe that the New Deal helped end the Depression. But there is substantial evidence that it might have helped *expand* the Depression. As historian Amity Shlaes argues in her book, *The Forgotten Man*, the New Deal had little impact in creating jobs and wealth for people.

When Shlaes' book was criticized for not counting the increase in government jobs in her research, the author responded by describing how she got her data:

A young economist named Stanley Lebergott helped the Bureau of Labor Statistics in Washington compile systematic unemployment data for that key period. He counted up what he called "regular work" such as a job as a school teacher or a job in the private sector. He intentionally did not include temporary jobs in emergency programs — because to count a short-term, make-work project as a real job was to mask the anxiety of one who really didn't have regular work with long-term prospects.

The result is what we today call the Lebergott/Bureau of Labor Statistics series. They show one man in four was unemployed when Roosevelt took office. They show joblessness overall always above the 14% line from 1931 to 1940. Six years into the New Deal and its programs to create jobs or help organized labor, two in 10 men were unemployed.

She also cites research performed at UCLA that found that by late 1939, total hours worked by the adult population was down by a fifth from ten years before.

"What kept the picture so dark so long?" Shlaes asks. "Deflation for one, but also the notion that government could engineer economic recovery by favoring the public sector at the expense of the private sector. New Dealers raised taxes again and again to fund spending. The New Dealers also insisted on higher wages when businesses could ill afford them. Roosevelt, for example, signed into law first his National Recovery Administration, whose codes forced businesses to pay an above-market minimum wage, and then the Wagner Act, which gave union workers more power."

The policies of the New Deal were designed to create jobs and wealth, and end the Depression. Shlaes believes these policies didn't work. Although laws such as the minimum wage did artificially inflate wages, these policies were ultimately counter-productive. "High wages hurt corporate profits and therefore hiring," Shlaes argues. "The unemployed stayed unemployed. 'If you had a job you were all right' — the phrase we all heard as children about the Depression — really does capture the period."

But it wasn't just historians looking back on the New Deal who realized that government couldn't provide jobs as the private sector could. There were many that made this very argument. One of these people was Wendell Willkie. He ran a utility company called Commonwealth & Southern and the goal was to create electricity throughout the South.

Yet FDR had other ideas. Under his leadership, the government created a counter to Commonwealth & Southern: the Tennessee Valley Authority (TVA). The result? Commonwealth & Southern suffered greatly as utility stocks barely moved during the 1930s. Not that the TVA was an economic juggernaut. It was a typical big government enterprise that was inefficient since it didn't have to compete on the same terms as private utilities. And so the New Deal created government enterprises that didn't work and hampered private enterprises from working as well as they could have.

In a famous radio address to the nation, Willkie challenged the New Deal and argued that it had made the Great Depression worse. "For several years now," Willkie lamented, "we have been listening to a bedtime story, telling us that the men who hold office in Washington are, by their very positions, endowed with a special virtue."

There was another side to Willkie. In *Five Days In Philadelphia* (the story of how Willkie switched from Democrat to Republican in 1939 and gave FDR the race of his life a year later), author Charles Peters notes that at the same time Willkie was crusading against TVA and New Deal regulators, "he was becoming known as a critic of industry abuses, particularly those of the holding companies that played a shell game with their assets, moving them from one state to another to stay one step ahead of both regulation and taxation."

Were Wendell Willkie here today, he would no doubt have some interesting things to say about the present state of government involvement in the market and about the abuses by industry itself.

Finally, the Great Depression ended, but not because of the New Deal. It ended when World War II created unprecedented demand for economic production.

And who was footing the bill for the ten year experiment of replacing private sector jobs with public sector jobs? Shlaes quotes scholar William Graham Sumner's essay on the Forgotten Man: "He works; he votes; generally, he prays — but he always pays."

And so it always is when the institution of government reaches beyond its purpose and assumes the role of another institution: the social experiment fails but leaves debt and squandered human potential in its wake. Big government has left a bill that our great grandchildren will not be able to pay. Our entire society is being impacted. And in more ways than just money, that bill is already beginning to come due.

Government and Society

FDR understood that the nation was facing an economic crisis. But the philosophy behind his policy was not a natural extension of the political philosophies of Locke, Rousseau, Jefferson, Adams, Washington and Kuyper. It was progressivism, which was an amalgam of fascist, communist and socialist thought. These ideologies were rooted in the evolution and theism popularized by Darwin and Karl Marx. FDR didn't understand that the natural extension of the freedoms described in our Constitution were the inalienable rights contained in Kuyper's cultural mandate. Had he understood this relationship, the government he implemented and his treatment of the business institution would have been much different, and the Great Depression would have ended sooner. Indeed, it is less accurate to say that WWII got us out of the Depression than it is to say that it was FDR's realization that he needed the institution of business to build an arsenal in defense of a growing threat overseas. It was his change of attitude toward the institution of business that ended the Great Depression.

In *The New Dealers War*, historian Thomas Fleming writes vividly of the wartime Congress creating a joint Committee on Unnecessary Government Expenditures and, in a short period, its penciling out funding for New Deal era domestic spending programs. Congress' purpose in so doing was obvious: in order to fund a war in two theatres, domestic spending had to be cut dramatically and defense spending had to rise dramatically as a portion of the Gross Domestic Product. Without exception, FDR signed the budgets that had defunded and eliminated the programs he had created in the previous decade. As the president himself put it on several occasions, "Dr. New Deal is retiring to make way for Dr. Win the War."

Subsequently, FDR's approach to business changed. He adopted free market principles that allowed industry to flourish. It was the adoption of these free market principles that began to lift us out of the Depression. But it is lamentable that it took a world war to change his economic agenda. Had the FDR of the 1930's concentrated on punishing those responsible for the Great Depression, enacted laws to prevent such severe crashes from happening again, and encouraged the free market, the Great Depression would have ended much sooner. The New Deal had the opposite effect, and the impacts of its implementation are being felt decades later.

The New Deal's affect on other institutions has been profound. It began the government's increasing (and unhealthy) expansion of power during the 20th Century.

Charles Kresler, a Government professor at Claremont McKenna, has described three waves of government expansion during the past one hundred years, and how each one chipped away at the foundations of America's institutions.

The progressives at the beginning of the 20th century saw expansion of government as the means through which the culture could be changed. The progressives "regarded the Constitution and the old forms of American politics as outmoded," says Kresler. Candidates promising to be good stewards of the public trust were replaced by a new political model. The progressives, especially Woodrow Wilson, began talking about having a "vision of the future" where government would enact new policies to deal with new problems. Government, instead of the people, would be the holder of political power.

According to Kresler, this political liberalism led directly to the economic liberalism of the 1930's, the second wave of government expansion. "A right to a job, a right to health care, a right to a home, a right to an education. All these things became as fundamental to liberals as the rights to 'life, liberty and the pursuit of happiness' that we find in the Declaration of Independence," Kresler says.

One almost-forgotten-but-recently revived fact is that a Second Bill of Rights was actually proposed by President Franklin D. Roosevelt in his State of the Union address on January 11, 1944. Maintaining that the Constitution and the Bill of Rights had "proved inadequate to assure us equality in the pursuit of happiness," FDR called for "an economic bill of rights" to guarantee Americans: a job with a "living wage;" freedom from monopolies and unfair competition; a home; and health care; education; and Social Security.

The revival of the Second Bill of Rights occurred during the health care debate of 2009-2010, as proponents of universal health care made the argument that every American is entitled to health care. In addition, Cass Sunstein, former Harvard professor and the regulation czar in the Obama White House, has written extensively in favor of FDR's "Second Bill of Rights." As Sunstein is increasingly mentioned for higher positions within the Administration, there is fresh focus on his writings on this area.

Finally, in the 1960's, President Johnson's Great Society became the third wave of government expansion. This wave was accompanied by a cultural liberalism that, as Kresler notes, redefined freedom to mean the "freedom of liberation, which is really freedom from responsibilities." Government expansion and cultural liberalism locked arms and marched the country toward a brave, new world.

Politically, economically and culturally, the influence of the Government Institution has grown by leaps and bounds, far removed from the limited government created by the Founding Fathers.

On January 20, 2009, an historic inauguration took place. Barack Obama became the first African-American president of the United States. Republicans and Democrats together celebrated this remarkable achievement, believing it to be the final chapter in the sad saga of racial discrimination against blacks in America.

Obama became the 44th President at a time when many Americans were tired of a controversial war and we were facing the most uncertain and alarming times since the Great Depression. The Obama era marked the end of the Republican era of the Contract With America and the Bush presidency's broken promise to reduce the size of government.

With a sense of hope in the air, most Americans were excited about this new Administration, hoping for a moderate president who would guide us out of our economic woes. But others believed it would take months to determine from where on the political spectrum this president would govern. Would he be a centrist or govern from the extreme liberal left?

Only three months before, Treasury officials rushed to Capitol Hill to say a world-wide market crash was upon us unless Congress immediately gave them a $700 billion-plus bailout package with no strings attached. With restrictions, the bill was passed and bloated the budget of '08 from around $2.2 trillion to more than $2.9 trillion. During the Bush years (2001—09), public spending increased by 70 percent, more than double the increase in spending under President Clinton (1993-2001). The annual deficits for the previous five years began at $400 billion in 2004, then dropped down for a couple of years, and then mushroomed close to $500 billion in 2008.

With a "stimulus" package of $800 billion-plus, a budget that ballooned to $3.5 trillion in 2009, a resulting deficit projected at $2 trillion, a plan that would enhance the government's hand in health care at a level previously unreached, and a proposal to deal with global warming (now increasingly called "climate change") that many feared would lead to an electricity tax that would hit hardest at lower-income Americans, it became clear that President Obama, House Speaker Nancy Pelosi and Senate Majority Leader Harry Reid were advancing a far left agenda. The agenda they put forth and enacted in Congress was in no way shape, or form, centrism.

This troika was blind to the lessons of the Great Depression. They did not learn from history. It was said that the "stimulus" bill was needed to keep unemployment below 8% with claims that, upon enactment of this bill, unemployment would be lowered by 2 percentage points. As of this writing, about half of the stimulus money has gone into government-backed programs and none directly to private industry. With the unemployment hovering at the same rate as it was before the stimulus package was enacted into law, this is evidence that the program for recovery is not working.

The "roadmap" of deficit spending to alleviate economic recession is not new. Neither is the fact that some politicians have not learned the sad lessons from this disastrous course. But there are some who have and are willing to admit the errors of their past ways. Such as Colorado's former three-term Gov. Richard Lamm who, in 1988, created a stir when he came out foursquare in favor of a Balanced Budget Amendment to the Constitution. As a liberal Democrat who had long championed the idea of government intervention and spending, Lamm seemed an unlikely champion for fiscal belt-tightening. But, likening himself to Saul of Tarsus on the road to Damascus, Lamm told an interviewer: "I read [economist John Maynard] Keynes and knew about deficit spending in times of recession and depression. But Keynes also said that once the crisis has passed, the deficit spending must cease. I did not follow all of what Keynes advised while I was governor. And I was wrong."

Sadly, there are too few like Lamm in positions of power today. And the individual is paying the price. And, as a result, the other institutions outside of government are being destroyed.

Americans are astonished at the direction this Administration is taking and astounded by the runaway spending. The Republican era failed to limit government during times of economic prosperity. This new Democrat era will bring about limited government by collapsing under unsustainable debt.

Government and the Individual

In his book, "The Prayer of Jabez," author Bruce Wilkinson tells the story of a Mr. Jones who dies and goes to heaven. Upon his arrival, he is met at the gates by Saint Peter, who gives him a tour. There is a particular building that Mr. Jones asks about. Saint Peter takes him into it. There, Mr. Jones sees packages neatly gift-wrapped. "Do I have a package in there?" he asks. Peter responds: "Yes you do." Sure enough, Mr. Jones finds a box with his name on it. He opens it and he is shocked by what he sees, Wilkinson writes, "Because there in Mr. Jones's white box are all the blessings that God wanted to give him while he was on earth... but Mr. Jones never asked." This story has great relevance to our discussion.

When the institution of government expands beyond the purpose for which it was created, people become confused as to where to look for help. Rather than look to themselves, they look to government. Rather than seek out friends and family, they seek out a federal program. Rather than ask God for help, they ask Washington for money. For too many, it is easier to look to Washington than look for a job. When any of the four institutions expand beyond the purpose for which it was created, the functioning of the other institutions are impaired.

The Government institution was never intended and never designed to be all things to all people. We were designed by a God who protects and provides through the four institutions. Each institution has a distinct purpose and function. But all are necessary for the abundant life God wants us to have. Each of us has a right to access all of these institutions.

But since the New Deal, government has encouraged the idea that all wisdom flows from the Potomac River in Washington. Despite the evidence that this has had disastrous results for our families and our country, too many Americans still want government to do more than it should.

In his book, *The Tragedy of American Compassion*, Marvin Olasky criticized American welfare policy because it provided the wrong kind of charity. He points to charity in the 1800's as being a better model because it usually came from a church or private organization. And this kind of charity to the poor almost always involved the direct involvement of its members. This human interaction made a huge difference both for the giver and recipient. Olasky argued that government programs can't re-create this personal engagement and instead creates a distance between those receiving help and those paying for it.

Olasky also argued that private charity is different from that provided by government because it asks something from the receiver. Those who get help from a church are often asked to find jobs or clean up their lives to lead a more abundant life that can be accessed through the three other institutions. This is real change and a far cry from the dependency fostered through government largesse. When government invaded the province of privately-run charities, it proceeded to cause new, unforeseen problems for those receiving the benefits. It also had the potential to damage private programs.

In 1931, Congress voted down a measure to provide the Red Cross with $25 million in tax dollars for food. This would be the first time anyone proposed giving the respected charity organization any federal dollars. The Hoover Administration opposed the measure, as did Red Cross President John Payne, who vowed that his organization would refuse the money if Congress appropriated it. House Majority Leader John Q. Tilton declared at the time: "Once the Red Cross is destroyed, as it must inevitably be by a federal dole, and our local charities paralyzed, as they will be when the federal government takes over responsibility for charitable relief, the appropriations that must follow as a consequence of such policy would stagger belief." The great progressive movement of the 1930's overwhelmed this sentiment. By 1935, the Red Cross was accepting federal dollars and was, in fact, the only organization designated by Congress to deal with disaster relief.

In his study of the Red Cross for the Capital Research Center, Martin Morse Wooster noted that "Red Cross disaster relief planners cut down their estimates of how long it would take a community to recover from a disaster. . . . In 1969, the Red Cross changed its rules so that all aid was dispensed according to a mathematical formula that left no room for discretion. The decades-old practice of investigating each case ended."

"In the 1960's," Wooster wrote, "the massive expansion of the welfare state meant more government grants and contracts for faith-based non-profits and the Salvation Army expanded its disaster relief efforts to the extent that it became the alternative national disaster agency. The Army formally became a component of the federal government's national disaster plans, although less so than the Red Cross."

Majority Leader Tilton was prescient as what happened to the Salvation Army and the Red Cross would show. Red Cross spokesman Donald Coble told the *New York Times:* "We've been bumping into each other and we're trying to get away from it—it can be quite expensive. We've had cases of people getting clothing from one organization and then getting the same thing from another."

Wooster pointed out that the Salvation Army also paid a price of its own for accepting tax-funded growth. "The Army is both a church and a non-profit," he wrote, "and until federal funds began to come in, the Army put no barriers between its dual roles." But as the federal largesse began to flow in large amounts during the 1970's, the tensions between the Army's social service programs and its evangelism "had become acute and remained so" for decades, observed historian E.H. McKinley. Because of its acceptance of federal grants, the Salvation Army was forced "to divide its programs for budgetary purposes into 'religious' and 'social activities,' which was distasteful to them and antithetical to the Army's longstanding tradition that its social and spiritual work could not be divided." In a nutshell, that was the cost to private charities for welcoming the federal government and its tax dollars.

The federal government can only print money; it can't change lives.

This became evident again in a recent report commissioned by the YMCA, Dartmouth Medical School and the Institute for American Values. Called "Hardwired to Connect: The New

Scientific Case for Authoritative Communities," the report was written by 33 experts with experience in fields ranging from pediatric medicine to mental health to youth services.

The report diagnosed a serious problem facing the next generation of Americans. The report stated: "We are witnessing high and rising rates of depression, anxiety, attention deficit, conduct disorders, thoughts of suicide, and other serious mental, emotional, and behavioral problems among U.S. children and adolescents."

The cause for this epidemic?

According to the report, "In large measure, what's causing this crisis of American childhood is a lack of connectedness. We mean two kinds of connectedness — close connections to other people, and deep connections to moral and spiritual meaning."

The report goes on to state that connectedness comes from interaction with "social institutions" that provide young people with purpose. But these institutions are growing weaker, not stronger, according to the report, "social institutions that foster these two forms of connectedness for children have gotten significantly weaker." That weakening, this report argues, is a major cause of the current mental and behavioral health crisis among U.S. children.

The New World Order is the Old World Order

Simply put, the major institutions of our faith, family and work have been weakened and children are paying the price. In fact, the family institution is broken, and kids are reeling from the resulting dysfunction. The institution of Government has been very effective at one thing: undermining the other institutions.

Is it any wonder that individuals—especially young people—are struggling to find connectedness and purpose in their lives? "Where is the life we have lost in living?" the poet T.S. Eliot wrote. Indeed, in the face of expanded government programs with names like "The Great Society" and "The New Deal," individual purpose and meaning have been compromised.

It is time to restore the institution of Government to its proper role.

Chapter Seven

A New Social Contract

The Pursuit of Happiness and the Four Institutions

When Americans talk about the Founding Fathers today, they often speak of them as gods or at least demigods. And the Constitution often takes on a spiritual quality in the minds of many Americans.

All well and good, but as Richard Beeman discusses in his new book, *Plain, Honest Men: The Making of the American Constitution*, the Founding Fathers were not gods. And their creation was by no means perfect.

The challenge facing the men at Philadelphia was to repair the Articles of Confederation. Crafted in 1777 and finally ratified by the thirteen colonies, the Articles were a well-intentioned document with which to govern the infant nation, but they had several flaws: a Congress with one representative from each state, thus creating tension between the more and less populous states; a rotating chief executive, with the nation having ten chief executives for its eight years under the Confederation; and much of the power going to states rather than the federal government. The "Shay's Rebellion" would reveal the weakness of this fragmentation of power. When debtors in Massachusetts were being jailed for refusal to pay back taxes and debts to the state, a Revolutionary War veteran named Daniel Shays launched a rebellion in the spirit of the American Revolution itself. Because the power of the states trumped that of the federal government, there was little the nation's Congress could do about the more than 1000 rebel debtors imprisoned by the state before it was over (the Shay's Rebellion also sparked the now-famous comment by Thomas Jefferson, then U.S. ambassador to France, to a friend that he wasn't bothered by the uprising because "a little rebellion now and then is a good thing.") But the uprising did lead Alexander Hamilton and other Founding Fathers to conclude that the Confederation government had little means to deal with crisis situations in the 13 states and that a new government was needed. "Something drastic needed to be done to save their experiment in liberty and union," Beeman says in his book.

And as representatives of the states met in Philadelphia in 1787, their goal was not to provide a perfect document that could foresee the future, but to deal with the recent past and immediate present. To redress the weaknesses inherent in the Articles of Confederation, the Constitution that emerged from Philadelphia was designed to create a stronger federal government to promote law and order while simultaneously preserving the liberties of the people.

The Constitution worked and solved the problems of the 18th century. But it had to be amended to address seemingly intransigent issues, most famously slavery, which the Founding Fathers left in place. Still, there have been only 27 amendments in 213 years and that shows impressively the efficacy of the original document. But the amendment process was created by the men in Philadelphia precisely to deal with new situations and changing times.

Thus, Beeman argues that Founding Father Robert Morris correctly judged the Constitution as being far from a miracle document. "While some have boasted it as a work from Heaven, others have given it a less righteous origin. I have many reasons to believe that it is the work of plain, honest men."

Those plain, honest men gave us a great, divinely inspired government. Certainly not perfect, as no act of man can be, their work will always be recognized as a giant leap forward for freedom and liberty.

The Founding Fathers of the 18th century could not have envisioned what the country would face in the 21st century. They never experienced an $800 billion stimulus package from the government, or Bernie Madoff business deals, or a divorce rate of 50%, or churches spending more money on new sanctuary buildings than helping the poor. They never lived through a Great Depression or "did" the cultural 1960's as hippies or flower children. But they were cognizant of the threat posed by a more than limited government. Concerned about the mindset of his generation led Thomas Paine to say they live on "confounding government with society, so as to leave little distinction between the two." The distinction is even less defined now, and the stakes are much higher.

Given today's move to make the Constitution a "living" document, and the liberal interpretation of the welfare clause and the massive federal government it has created, it is impossible to return government to the minimalist vision of the Founding Fathers without the illumination and application of the Cultural Mandate—a nation living in freedom and liberty in the face of God with unfettered access to the four institutions.

In the Declaration of Independence, Jefferson wrote that the new nation would be devoted to "life, liberty and the pursuit of happiness." Perhaps it's time to look at how the Four Institutions of the Cultural Mandate apply to the pursuit of happiness.

Maybe it is time to "unconfound," government and society once and for all with a post American Founding political philosophy that is a natural extension of Natural Law. And the key will be to clarify and promote the third of Jefferson's promises: the pursuit of happiness.

The pursuit of happiness described by our Founding Fathers has its fullest expression in the Four Institutions of the Cultural Mandate. In the Garden we lived "in the face of God." We were free and had liberty. Happiness was achieved by living as intended: in fellowship with God, building families and tending the Garden. The freedom and liberty secured by our forefathers was an enormous step toward what will someday be access to these four institutions established in the beginning of time.

The directives of the Cultural Mandate define inalienable rights in the pursuit of happiness:

The right to love God above all things and the right to love our neighbor as ourselves

The right to a mother and a father

The right to a vocation

The right to protection under the law

If we have the inalienable right to the pursuit of happiness, and happiness is achieved through these four institutions, then we have an inalienable right of access to these four institutions. They are the means by which we are allowed to achieve happiness. But, in America today, the institutions are being destroyed. The mushrooming of big government at the federal level is destroying our access to the full, free exercise of religion, our right to a mother and father and to a vocation.

The door to the federal government as the first resource for relief and assistance was opened early in the 20th Century and, since then, government has become pervasive. The more it expands, the more it prevents access to the other institutions for more and more Americans. "As government expands, liberty contracts," Ronald Reagan warned. And he was right.

How do we restore and secure theses rights for all Americans? Certainly not by the government expansion that began in the 1930's and continues to this day by leaders in Washington. The FDR/Obama social contract was and is based on ideas that swarmed Europe and America in the early 20th century. In fashion during this period was the use of Darwin's evolutionary paradigm as the "scientific" rationale for statism. Armed with Darwin's "proof" that God was dead, Marxism found a far less cluttered path to initiate an era of strong and brutal centrally controlled governments. The evils of fascism, communism and socialism ushered in during this period stood in stark contrast to the liberty and freedom that formed the foundation of this country and of the freedoms of the Cultural Mandate.

These philosophies continue to threaten freedom. Remnants of communism, socialism, fascism, and the ideas behind these "movements," are a threat to the American Example, the American Experiment and American Exceptionalism. They burrow into the public psyche during times of national instability, when greed, stupidity and arrogance make the normal ups and downs of business cycles swing high and crash dramatically. As is now clearly evident, these ideas bankrupt the country and rob Americans of their freedom.

In his book, *Liberal Fascism*, Jonah Goldberg writes:

> As liberalism in recent years has fallen into ideological and intellectual disarray, American liberals have crouched into a fetal position around Franklin D. Roosevelt's "legacy." Liberal legal theorists have made the New Deal into a second American founding. Leading journalists have descended into abject idolatry. Indeed, it sometimes seems that all one needs to know about the merits of a policy is whether Roosevelt himself would have favored it. It is a given that Republicans are wrong, even fascistic, whenever they want to "dismantle" FDR's policies.
>
> One of the most poignant ironies here is that a modern-day Hitler or Mussolini would never dismantle the New Deal. To the contrary, he'd redouble the effort. This is not to say the New Deal was evil or Hitlerian. But the New Deal was a product of the impulses and ideas of its era. And those ideas and

impulses are impossible to separate from the fascist moment in Western civilization. According to Harold Ickes, FDR's Interior secretary and one of the most important architects of the New Deal, Roosevelt himself privately acknowledged that "what we were doing in this country were some of the things that were being done in Russia and even some of the things that were being done under Hitler in Germany. But we were doing them in an orderly way." It's hard to see how orderliness absolves a policy from the charge of fascism or totalitarianism. Eventually, the similarities had become so transparent that Ickes had to warn Roosevelt that the public was increasingly inclined "to unconsciously group four names, Hitler, Stalin, Mussolini and Roosevelt."

The notion that FDR harbored fascist tendencies is vastly more controversial today than it was in the 1930's, primarily because fascism has come to mean Nazism and Nazism means simply evil. Saying, for example, that FDR had a Hitlerite fiscal policy just confuses people. But the fascist flavor of the New Deal was not only regularly discussed; it was often cited as evidence in Roosevelt's favor.

Indeed, the New Deal was conceived at the climax of a worldwide fascist moment, a moment when socialists in many countries were increasingly becoming nationalists and nationalists could embrace nothing other than socialism. Franklin Roosevelt was no fascist, at least not in the sense that he thought of himself in this way. But many of his ideas and policies were indistinguishable from fascism. And today we live with the fruits of fascism, and we call them liberal.

These old ideas continue to stand in stark contrast to the wisdom of the Founding Fathers and the happiness found in the four institutions of the Cultural Mandate. The chasm between the two competing world views cannot be bridged. We need a new social contract to replace socialisms "cradle to grave" contract.

However, a new social contract for America cannot begin with government; it must begin with society, our culture. We, the People, "us guys." Making access to these four institutions available to all Americans will direct us in reducing the size of government. What is needed, in effect, is a reconnection and reaffirmation to those four great institutions which made government minimal and responsible at the same time. The institutions established at the beginning of time and the limited powers established by the Constitution of the United States of America will guide us to a restoration of the American Dream.

New Contract

The institutions of family, faith and work will reclaim their proper roles of preparation, persuasion and provision in American society. Individual Americans, from the wealth generated by the institution of business, will contribute to private organizations that care for the poor and needy. These organizations will take all charity and its distributions away from government. Private funds directed through these faith based organizations will be directed at rebuilding the American family. Government will return to its proper role of protection by capping federal spending, reforming entitlement programs and assisting people in their move from dependence to independence.

With the four institutions engaged in their proper roles and with an allegiance to the United States Constitution we can work together to rebuild and restore America.

CHAPTER EIGHT

Implementing the Contract

For years, Don Eberly has studied the relationship between culture and politics. He has been a staffer in the U.S. Congress, director of the House Republican Study Committee, head of the Commonwealth Foundation in Pennsylvania and held high-ranking positions under two Presidents. Eberly has been inside the corridors of power. But as a scholar, he's also studied the limits of politics and the importance of culture. He describes what he found:

> Law, in the end, is downstream from the culture. When the mores shift, the laws almost inevitably shift along with them. Edmund Burke said that manners are more important than laws because upon manners in great measure the laws depend. Plato said, give

me the songs of a nation—it matters not who writes the laws. We must conclude, as Wilberforce concluded, that if we are going to change law, we must go upstream to the tributaries of moral beliefs and conduct. In doing so we must understand that this work will not be done by the state but will be done by various voluntary associations within civil society.

The solution to America's problems today will emerge as a result of understanding this truth: that culture is upstream from law, politics and jurisprudence. Rather than Washington changing America, Americans must change America, and then Washington will follow. Fortunately, we have examples that will help lead the way.

Outclass Government

Most of the sites we see in Washington, DC were created by the federal government: the National Mall, the various monuments, the Capitol, the White House. But one of the greatest sites in Washington was the creation of one man: Andrew Mellon.

Mellon had served as Treasury Secretary and was one of the wealthiest men in America. But in addition to making money, he collected art. And as the Great Depression deepened in the 1930s, Mellon purchased more and more art at falling prices. But rather than horde this collection, Mellon wanted to share it with the country. He envisioned creating a national gallery in Washington, DC. But more important than *what* he wanted to do, was *why* he wanted to do it. Amity Schlaes explains Mellon's motivation behind this effort in her book, *The Forgotten Man:*

> But what was new was something that Mellon was only now revealing—what had been on his mind all these years, the philosophy behind the donation of the collection. Mellon was not trying to bribe the government, or even placate it. He was trying to outclass it.
>
> For years he had tried to show, through business, that the private sector could give to the people, just as government could, and sometimes more. Then he had tried to demonstrate the same thing from his post at Treasury, through his tax cuts. Now, pleased but

still not satisfied with his work through the first two methods, he was trying a third: charity.

In Mellon's head, the plan was entirely clear. By giving largely, generously, completely, and entirely, he would demonstrate that the private man could be as good a servant to the public as the government official was—certainly, he was ahead of [his successor as secretary of the treasury, Henry] Morgenthau. What's more, he would make his gift selflessly. It would not bear his name: 'It shall be known as the National Gallery of Art or by such other name as may appropriately identify it...' Even the display of the paintings would be unselfish—they would be arranged by period and style, not by collector or collection.

In the middle of the New Deal, with stunning and enormous government expansion, one man wanted to make a statement – that people, not government, could make the greater difference. People could outclass government. And so, one of the world's greatest art museums was created, not only to showcase the beauty of art, but to showcase the power of the private sector. More specifically, it was built to demonstrate the power of a single businessman determined to impact the public good.

Andrew Mellon proved that the private sector can strengthen and improve the country better than the government can. Today's Andrew Mellon's need to outclass government again, by capitalizing a private national fund for the specific purpose of rebuilding our decayed institutions.

Rekindle The Independence Machine

"How can I help this man?" thought Father Daniel Coughlin, chaplain of the U.S. House of Representatives, when he watched a certain congressman from California address the president and members of the House and Senate at a Republican retreat at the Greenbrier in West Virginia.

It was 2002. President George W. Bush was riding high in the polls and the Republican Party was riding high with him. Unemployment was low. The nation was responding decisively to 9/11. In January, the president said the state of the union was strong. But something was missing. The country's wealth was not reflective of the country's health. More and more, America seemed to be a society that knew the cost of everything and the value of nothing. So I decided to speak up.

I told the President about a joint House-Senate resolution I was co-sponsoring with Harold Ford, Jr. in the House along with senators Santorum and Lieberman in the Senate. Ford was a Democratic member from Tennessee and an African-American, Rick Santorum of Pennsylvania, a conservative Republican, and Joe Lieberman of Connecticut, a centrist Democrat who only two years before had been his party's nominee for vice president (and who four years later would be rejected by his party for renomination for the Senate but re-elected as an independent). The sponsors of the resolution covered all parts of the political spectrum.

The resolution's premise was simple: if the national charitable giving rate was increased just one percent, from its historical rate of 1.5 to 2% annually, to 3%, it would provide more than $100 billion every year to churches and non-profit organizations all across America. The number was significant and the wheels clearly began turning in the president's mind, thinking of the impact this could have on America.

The president responded, "It would be very tough for me, as president, to ask people to give more." He was right. With rampant government spending and the current tax burden, most Americans would not be responsive to any government official, even the president, asking them to give more to charity. Put another way, with 40% of tax payer income going to support government at the state, local, and federal level, and public debt on the rise, it would be difficult to ask the tapped-out taxpayers to give even more.

My idea left an impression, but the president and the Republican Congress were still clinging to the notion that Republicans, while in the majority, were going to solve all the nation's problems the old fashioned way, from inside the Beltway.

But if it didn't make a strong impact on the president, it did with the chaplain. Father Coughlin understood the impact Americans could have by giving more to and strengthening the private sector. At a meeting with me later in the chaplain's office in the United States Capitol, he and I discussed strategies for moving the issue forward. He recalled hearing my question to the president at the Greenbrier and wondered how he could help with the resolution I had co-sponsored.

Father Coughlin agreed to take the resolution to the National Council of Catholic Bishops to get its support. The result? They rejected the idea outright. Why? Because of one small statement in the Resolution. The non-binding resolution included the following language, "*Whereas a one percent increase in charitable giving may reduce the federal deficit...*" [Emphasis added].

With forty percent of Catholic Charities funded by government, the Council of Bishops did not want to risk their government funding by asking people to give more to the church! This is not just true of the Catholic Church, but of most large religious organizations in the United States. This sentiment lies at the root of the general misunderstanding of the proper roles of the four institutions.

The institution of faith is part of the solution, but sometimes it becomes part of the problem as seen by the example described above. For decades, various sectors of American life have been seduced, subdued and then neutered by the government. Businesses were offered subsidies; families were offered tax credits. But the seduction of faith was the worst and most damaging of all. The one institution that can play a leading role in righting the ship of culture by the power of persuasion instead is helping to swamp it.

Now would be a good time to consider these quotes on virtue and liberty compiled and edited by J. David Gowdy, President of The Washington, Jefferson & Madison Institute:

The New World Order is the Old World Order

"Can it be that Providence has not connected the permanent felicity of a nation with its virtue?"

George Washington

"The only foundation of a free Constitution is pure Virtue, and if this cannot be inspired into our People, in a great Measure, than they have it now. They may change their Rulers, and the forms of Government, but they will not obtain a lasting Liberty.

John Adams

"Only a virtuous people are capable of freedom. As nations become more corrupt and vicious, they have more need of masters."

Benjamin Franklin

"When virtue is banished, ambition invades the minds of those who are disposed to receive it, and avarice possesses the whole community."

Montesquieu

(written by Thomas Jefferson in his *Common Place Book*).

"To suppose that any form of government will secure liberty or happiness without any virtue in the people, is a chimerical idea."

James Madison

Why was virtue considered by our Founding Fathers to be so important to lasting liberty, fidelity and freedom? Because a constitutional government based on the consent of the governed relies on the strength and viability of the other institutions in society in order for it to last. The most critical of these is the faith institution, of which the promotion of virtue is a vital characteristic. Faith fuels true charity and undergirds the moral imperatives of family and work. Government cannot define and force civil virtue, it can only defend it.

Therefore, a strong faith institution is the key to a free culture and society.

Consider this Biblical perspective written by the apostle Peter. "And beside this, giving all diligence, add to your faith virtue; and to virtue knowledge; and to knowledge temperance; and to temperance patience; and to patience godliness; and to godliness brotherly kindness; and to brotherly kindness charity."(2 Peter 1: 5-7). Peter's instructions do not provide a role for government in promoting virtue and its resulting attributes.

Virtue is a product of faith, but it leads on to much, much more. The journey from faith to godliness is a manifestation, or the product, of loving God above all else. As we move through Peter's process, godliness leads to brotherly kindness and charity. When we are free to exercise our right to love God above all things, godliness comes into our lives and, along with it, independence and self-determination. Just as important, though, is the freedom faith brings to love our neighbor as ourselves and the change in society that that love produces. Charity begets faith again, coupled with the personal responsibility it leads to, begins the movement of our population from dependence to independence. Faith is a "machine of independence."

Whether they knew it or not, the founding fathers reference to virtue was recognition of faiths role in building the other institutions necessary for a free society to succeed. This is what lifts the United States of America, along with the rest of the world, out of tyranny and on to freedom.

The time has come to repurpose the Faith Institution. It's time for this institution to shed its dependence on government assistance and build a new alliance with the Business

Institution to fund life changing charity. In real charity is found the perfect manifestation of the horizontal relationships mandated by God, which are the result of the individual's vertical relationship with Him. And with wise expenditures of private funds the work of rebuilding the American family can begin.

Leaders of all faiths must swear off government aid and, with the help of those who generate wealth in America, begin anew under the banner of true love and charity, helping to move Americans from dependency to independence. Faith that builds independence and self-determination can lead the world from tyranny to freedom.

Rebuild the Family

Earlier I wrote about Daniel Patrick Moynihan's insight in the 1960's. He proclaimed that poverty doesn't create broken families, but that broken families do create poverty. The key to turning the country around both economically and socially is to rebuild the family, and benefactors of the business institution and faith organizations can do this. Government cannot.

Proceeding every era of government expansion is a significant failure of the business institution. The Four Horsemen of Wall Street—Greed, Mendacity, Stupidity and Arrogance—create social instability, and unnecessarily wide swings in the marketplace. Government runs to the rescue, buying off one constituency group after another with large sums of money and the promise it can make our lives better. Then the cultural "revolution" collapses the family structure, aiding and abetting government expansion with more promises for a brighter future.

Vulnerable children form the foundation of the American culture of dependence, which is perpetuated by a trend toward more government involvement in the market place and individual lives. The latest example of this government intrusion being the health care measure enacted by Congress and signed into law by the president in 2010.

Rebuilding the American family will take more than just changing laws such as no-fault divorce and establishing a tax policy respecting families. It will take more to encourage families to stick together. It will take genuine outreach by faith institutions and business who believe in genuine faith and true charity. Financing this outreach must come from those who generate wealth in America and create private sector jobs. The Andrew Mellons of today must step up to the plate and establish a fund to end government charity and rebuild the family through faith institutions.

It must begin with a well-funded, reengaged faith institution fully prepared to exercise its role of persuading Americans to move from dependence to independence. Through this persuasion a new generation will be built, and the American family rebuilt. The cycles of teenage pregnancy and divorce will be broken and fatherlessness addressed. Broken, fatherless families breed broken kids. Healing must begin with the fatherless.

As mentioned earlier, Art Rolnick, a Senior Vice President at the Federal Reserve Bank of Minneapolis, has a plan to do just that. His plan is to create an endowment fund to help disadvantaged children receive early childhood education. Specifically, families with an annual income of less than 185% of the Federal Poverty Guideline, about $40,000 for a family of four, would qualify. The program could be national and private; funded only by business and personal wealth, and administered through faith based organizations. So what would it take to fund this program?

Art began by starting a program in Minnesota in 2008. Although it is supported by a mixture of private and public funds, it provides families with information and resources to help them choose, pay for, and stay in high-quality early childhood education (ECE) programs. The ECE programs can use scholarship resources to increase and sustain quality programming.

A pregnant woman or a family with a child under one year of age is eligible to get a parent mentor. The parent mentor continues to visit until the child enters kindergarten. When the child reaches three years of age, he or she receives a two-year scholarship to pay for full- or part-time, center- or family-based early childhood education services.

A similar program is headed up by the Reverend Larry Arce at the Fresno Rescue Mission, although theirs is smaller and privately funded. Fatherless children and their mothers are given shelter, work and child care in order to learn a job skill within two years. Participants must foreswear government assistance before joining.

This program is the opposite of current federal programs. It does not incentivize single parenthood. It breaks the cycle of dependency. These programs offer real-life mentors, whereas federal programs offer money. Nothing can replace the impact that a caring human being can have on another person.

The private portion of funding for Art Rolnick's project in Minnesota comes from businessmen and businesswomen who see the long term economic benefits of fewer social services, more individualism and an expanded market base. It is considered a good long-term investment. Art estimates that it would take about $6 billion per year to fund a national program to reach every fatherless child in America. A capital fund of $350 billion would fund this annual expense. That may seem a heavy lift for the private sector. Consider this sum, however, in relation to the following:

- Individuals give almost $300 billion per year to private charities.

- $350 billion is only .002% of the Gross Domestic Product (GDP) of $14.6T (according to the International Monetary Fund).

- $350 billion is only .0875% of the total assets of member firms of the New York Stock Exchange NYSE ($4.145Trillion according to the NYSE Member Firm Report of 2010).

- $350 billion is only .002% of the total assets of the United States of America ($180Trillion according to the Federal Reserve Board, in their document Z1: Flow of Funds of the United States of America).

- Ending state sponsored government charity, financed by the taxpayer, would release upwards of $800 billion per year for use in the private sector.

Imagine the transformation of our federal welfare programs, which cost up to 25% of our federal budget, into a privately-funded Rolnick-style mentoring program? This can be accomplished in every community in America. This program will deliver a severe blow to fatherlessness in America, and, supplemented with communitywide efforts to dramatically reduce divorce and teenage pregnancy rates, we can rebuild the American family and stem the tide of government dependency. Not only would we save money, we would grow the economy, save lives and redeem the future of America.

Business and faith institutions can take charity away from government and rebuild the American family. But, eighty years of liberal progressivism and an entrenched government workforce will not let this happen without a fight – in the courts.

Obtain Standing in the Courts

In May 1954, the United States Supreme Court handed down one of its most significant, far-reaching, and controversial rulings in its history. In a case pitting civil rights activists against local Southern school districts, the court unanimously ruled that "separate but equal" was inherently unequal and the terms mutually exclusive. In so doing, the high court overruled its own 1896 ruling in *Plessy v. Ferguson*, which by a vote of 7-to-1 (with one abstention) upheld separate but equal accommodations. The 1954 ruling in *Brown vs. the Board of Education of Topeka*, sent shock waves across the country.

But those waves had been set in motion long before that day in 1954.

Since the end of Reconstruction following the Civil War, the South had fought back with "Jim Crow" laws that essentially established a caste system not unlike the apartheid (government-sanctioned segregation) of South Africa. African-Americans were told where to sit in theaters and on buses, which restrooms to use and where to go to school. Some African-Americans, including the early civil rights leader Booker T. Washington, urged those in their community to accept this and make the most of it.

As the 20th century entered its midway point, African-American leaders began to think differently. One of them was a young lawyer for the National Association for the Advancement of Colored People (NAACP) named Thurgood Marshall. Marshall believed that the key to ending Jim Crow and changing America was to find cases that he could take to court and win. He carefully researched the background of a case before he decided whether to take it on. He wanted cases where there was an obvious villain. Marshall's reasoning for this was simple: he knew he had to not only change the law, but change hearts and minds as well.

One day he was discussing strategy with a fellow African-American who told him he had heard a white man joke that he didn't support segregation, he supported slavery. "There's something to that," Marshall responded. He knew it would be a long process before he could change racist minds in America.

He began in the 1940's with a few court cases concerning graduate school and law school. And then he turned his attention to secondary education. Again, Marshall chose this strategically. He knew it would be helpful if children were obvious victims. Who could oppose little children being given the right to an education?

Along the way, he worked hard to build relationships with local officials and raise awareness about the issues. And he was careful not to antagonize his opponents.

Marshall and his cause were helped by some outside circumstances, including race riots in major cities in the 1940's. This was a sign that African Americans who had left the segregated South for the urban centers of the North to escape Jim Crow laws were growing impatient with being treated as second-class citizens in the North. During World War II, African Americans put aside their feelings about racial injustice and fought for their country heroically against Japan and Germany—but they were forced to do so in segregated armed forces. Many came home and felt something finally had to be done to change this situation. The popularity of motion pictures and of African American film stars such as Lena Horne appearing aside white film stars had an impact on Americans who felt they deserved equal billing in their everyday lives.

Outside circumstances helped expedite the cause of racial equality in the post-war United States, but the patience and legal acumen of Thurgood Marshall, and the *Brown* decision were the key catalysts in changing how America dealt with race.

In the end, when the *Brown* ruling came down, he had changed the law. But through his work leading up to the ruling, he had also begun to change hearts and minds. It was a long, hard fight. But he won it.

Marshall, of course, went on to become a federal judge, U.S. solicitor general, and the first African-American to serve on the Supreme Court. But he was best remembered for what he did as litigator and private citizen and, most importantly, successfully arguing the *Brown* case. His work shows us that campaigns can be waged today to change minds about other issues as well.

Today's Thurgood Marshalls need to wage a privately-funded campaign in the courts to end government charity based on its violation of the First Amendment right to the free exercise of religion: the right to love God above all else and the right to love your neighbor as yourself. It is possible because jurisprudence is downstream from culture.

Conclusion

When he exited the Constitutional Convention in 1787, Ben Franklin was asked by a citizen what form of government the delegates had decided to give the young country. "A republic," he responded, "if you can keep it."

We kept it for more than 200 years. We've become the most influential and powerful country the world has ever seen. Along the way we have become the example of liberty and freedom to countries around the world.

Someone once said that Americans are an exceptional people. I disagree. As individuals, we aren't any more exceptional than anyone else in the world. But, has America been given an exceptional role in mankind's rise from tyranny to freedom? Absolutely! The most exceptional! We have risen to the challenge and the world is better with the presence of the United States of America. American exceptionalism is real. But if we, as a culture or society, don't reject the destructive ways of progressivism and embrace the wisdom of the Cultural Mandate and its four institutions we will lose our exceptional role. The growth of government, the deterioration of other American institutions, and crushing national debt has put us in decline and threaten our American exceptionalism. The world can't afford this decline.

The Four Institutions is a new worldview for a country desperately in need of change. Here is a new political spectrum, providing a clear choice between the failed, bankrupting, humanistic, dependence creating ideas of fascism, communism, socialism, liberal progressivism on one hand, and living a life of freedom in the face of God with a Constitution of limited powers and free access to four strong institutions in the Pursuit of Happiness, on the other.

CPSIA information can be obtained at www.ICGtesting.com
265013BV00002B/6/P